Books by Volker Heide

No More Tears

God's Punch Line

The Key is Love

Let Go and Let God

Available on Amazon

In Paperback and Kindle

THE KEY IS LOVE

Volker Heide

King of Kings Publishing
Madison, Connecticut

For Ernestine

Foreword

These sermons were preached in the parish. They are offered here with the prayer that they may give you a living hope in Christ.

The good news of God declares you can have a new life in Jesus Christ. He is the Savior who deeply loves you.

These sermons look at many different Bible Readings, and you are encouraged to read the passages listed beforehand.

God's Word is powerful and effective. The Holy Scriptures declare that God loves you. He cares about you and promises to provide for all of your needs.

Let these sermons lead you deeper into the Word of God. Read the Bible every day and study the Scriptures. There, you will find the answers you are looking for.

In God's Word, you will find Christ. He is the Son of God who comes to you with mercy and grace. Trust in him and receive his gift of life. Put your hope in him and receive his peace and blessing.

8

THE KEY IS LOVE
Featuring:

Therefore, since we have been justified through faith, we have peace with God through our Lord Jesus Christ, through whom we have gained access by faith into this grace in which we now stand.

Moreover, we rejoice in the hope of the glory of God. Not only so, but we also rejoice in our sufferings, because we know that suffering produces perseverance, and perseverance produces character, and character, hope.

And hope does not disappoint us, because God has poured out his love into our hearts by the Holy Spirit, whom he has given us.

You see, at just the right time, when we were still powerless, Christ died for the ungodly.

God demonstrates his own love for us in this: While we were still sinners, Christ died for us.

Romans 5:1-8

Since you have been raised with Christ, set your hearts on things above, where Christ is seated at the right hand of God.

Set your minds on things above, not on earthly things. For you have died with Jesus on the cross, and your life is now hidden with Christ in God.

When Christ, who is your life, appears, then you also will appear with him in glory.

Colossians 3:1-4

+

Jesus said, "So do not worry, saying, 'What shall we eat?' or 'What shall we drink?' or 'What shall we wear?' For even the unbelievers run after all these things, and your heavenly Father knows that you need them.

But seek first God's kingdom and his righteousness, and all these things will be given to you as well. Therefore, do not worry about tomorrow, for tomorrow will worry about itself. Each day has enough trouble of its own."

Matthew 6:31-34

THAT DIRTY WATER: 2 Kings 5:1-14

Today, we hear the story of Naaman and Elisha. It is a story of faith and unbelief, a story of humility and pride. In the end, it is the story of how God reaches out to us in love. The Lord lays his healing and helping hands upon us, and we are cleansed, restored and made new.

Our story begins with Naaman. He is the commander of the army of the king of Syria. Naaman was a five-star general, a rich and powerful man. He was smart and intelligent. He was great and proud.

But there was a big problem. Naaman had leprosy, an incurable disease. Leprosy would progressively get worse and worse. It would damage muscles and nerves; it would eat away at the skin and flesh; it was an incredibly painful illness that had no cure.

Try and picture how Naaman must have felt. Try and imagine being trapped in this way. Imagine being struck and having no hope for the future. Imagine dealing every day with the continuous pain of this illness.

Often, we feel like Naaman. It may be a severe illness or a chronic health problem. It may be the death of a loved one. It may be family or marriage troubles.

Circumstances beyond our control can back us into a corner where we feel trapped and stuck. Sometimes, we feel like there is no hope. We struggle with our pain and hurt.

But watch what happens now. A young girl from Israel is serving in the household of Naaman. This young girl had been captured by the Syrian army on one of their raids into northern Israel.

She says to Naaman's wife, "You know what? Your husband should seek out the great prophet Elisha who lives in Samaria. Elisha could cure him of his leprosy."

This young girl from Israel offers hope to this Syrian family. She knew that the Lord God was at work through the prophet Elisha. She knew that with God of Israel there is always hope. With God, all things are possible.

Here is a great example of faith. Faith always looks to God. Faith believes and trusts that God is able to help. If there's a problem, take it to the Lord.

Now what's truly remarkable about this girl is her situation. She was also trapped and stuck. She was a slave who was forced to work for the enemy of Israel, the dreaded Syrians.

And yet, despite her dire circumstances, this girl kept her faith. In fact, she not only kept her faith in God alive, but she also reaches out and shares her faith with her captors. She has compassion for Naaman and his wife.

The girl says to them, "There is a great prophet in Samaria. He could cure Naaman of his illness." And Naaman is quick to respond. He will pretty much do just about anything to get some help. He immediately goes to his boss and asks for permission to travel to Israel.

The king of Syria says, "Yes, by all means, go! I'll give you a medical leave of absence. Go and find some help. I'll even send a letter to the king of Israel to explain the situation."

So Naaman departs for Israel. He takes plenty of money to pay the doctor's bill. No expense is too great. He takes about 750 pounds of silver, 150 pounds of gold and 10 sets of costly clothing. No expense is too great if he can find healing and help.

When the king of Israel received Naaman and read his letter of request, he became furious. He said to Naaman, "Exactly what powers do you think I have? Why do you think I am able to cure leprosy? What are you trying to pull here?"

The king of Israel freaks out. He thinks the king of Syria is trying to trap him with this strange request.

The king at this time was Joram. He viewed this whole situation with suspicion and paranoia. Joram was a rotten king and a real unbeliever. He totally rejected God's Word, and he especially hated Elisha the prophet.

Joram was like so many people today. He was unhappy and confused. He viewed everyone around him with suspicion and distrust. He questioned God's way, and he complained about his life all the time. Joram found fault with everyone around him. He was a totally negative person.

But when the prophet Elisha learned about Naaman's arrival and his request, he sent word to Joram saying, "What's wrong with you, anyway? Send Naaman to me. I'll show you that there is a prophet in Israel. I'll show you what God can do."

So Naaman travels down to see Elisha, and when the general arrived with all of his chariots and horses and his entire entourage of servants, Elisha sends out a single servant to him with a simple message, "Go and wash yourself in the Jordan River seven times and your flesh shall be restored."

Now it's Naaman's turn to freak out. He becomes furious. Being rich and powerful and coming from such a sophisticated background, Naaman stubbornly refuses to do this. He declares, "No way! I will never subject myself to such a humiliation."

Naaman even says, "Are not the waters of the Abana and Pharpar, the great rivers of Damascus, much better than the muddy waters of Israel? Why should I wash myself in the dirty waters of the Jordan River?"

Naaman stumbles at this simple command. His pride trips him up. He thought Elisha would do something spectacular for him, maybe run a CAT-scan or give him an MRI or something like that.

But here is a reminder that God's ways are not our ways. God's way leads through the dirty waters of the Jordan

The Lord God says to us, "This is the way to be saved. This is how I restore and make clean. Go and wash in that dirty water!"

Naaman refuses to listen to Elisha. But his servants go to him and say, "What's wrong with you, anyway? If the prophet had told you to go to the Mayo Clinic, you would have gladly travelled to Minnesota. But when he tells you to this simple thing, you balk and refuse. Why don't you stop being so stubborn, and try God's way for once?"

That's the key to it all. Why don't you try God's way? Why don't you just have a little faith that maybe God knows what he is doing? Why don't you just let go of your pride, and submit to God's will for your life?

That's what Naaman does in the end, and the results are amazing. He went down to the Jordan River and dipped himself seven times in that dirty water and his flesh was restored. He was cleansed of his leprosy and healed.

Here, we see God's power clearly at work. We see a simple washing that brings a miraculous regeneration.

(Here also is wonderful foreshadowing of God's power at work in Holy Baptism. The heavenly Father takes this simple action of washing with water and bestows his gift of spiritual healing.)

Faith accepts the dirty waters of God's ways, and faith enabled Naaman to receive God's gift of healing. The same is true for us. Faith receives the gift. Faith is that open hand which simply receives God's blessing.

This reminds me of all the people with leprosy that Jesus healed. For example, we hear of one leper who came up to Jesus and knelt before him.

This sick man knew that Christ has the power to heal him. He had faith. And so, he says to Jesus, "Lord, I know that if you are willing, you can make me clean."

And Christ is moved with compassion and mercy. He reaches out his hand and touches the leper. "I am willing," he says, "Be clean!" He extends that healing touch and speaks his Word and the leper is immediately cured. His leprosy left him, just like that!

In Christ, we see how the God of Israel comes to heal and to save us. The Son of God humbles himself and he becomes flesh and blood, just like us.

And consider how Jesus was baptized in the muddy waters of the Jordan River. Our Lord submitted to John's baptism so that he might become our servant and take our place. He enters those dirty waters for us.

Christ humbles himself in the most amazing way. He gives up his perfect life so that we might receive healing for our souls.

He takes upon himself the leprosy of our sins so that we might be cleansed and made whole. "Surely he took up our infirmities and carried our diseases." "By his wounds, we are healed."

The Son of God suffered the dirty water of the cross. He experienced our sickness, so that we might receive that healing touch of his love and grace. Now, we discover that our Lord is able to transform our leprosy of sin into eternal health and well being.

This is precisely what we have received in Holy Baptism. Those simple waters were applied to us in the name of the Father and of the Son and of the Holy Spirit.

God's way leads us from the cross of Jesus to the waters of baptism. We wash ourselves in those simple waters and discover we are transformed and renewed and made whole. Sins are washed away by water and the Word. "For you have been born again, not of perishable seed, but of imperishable, through the living and enduring Word of God."

That is surprising. Perhaps we would have expected something else, something more spectacular and dramatic. God's ways seem so quaint and old-fashioned. His ways seem strange and odd.

That's how it seemed to Naaman, and that's how it seems to us today, too. It seems like God's ways are foolish and crazy. Why should I humiliate myself by washing in the muddy waters of the Jordan? Are not the clear waters of the Abana and Pharpar much better?

It is surprising to me that we Americans have one of the highest standards of living of any people on earth, and yet we are such an unhappy and discontented lot.

We have affluence and everything that money can buy, and yet, like king Joram, we are unhappy and confused. We find fault with everyone and everything around us.

And we are suspicious of God's ways. We are filled with such doubt and uncertainty. Our life is a mess and we are bitter and angry about it.

But could part of the problem be that we have rejected God? We insist on going our own way, and we come up empty. We try everything we can think of to fix our lives, and it never seems to work out.

What's wrong with us, anyway? Why don't we give God's way a try? Why don't we just have a little faith that maybe God knows what he is doing?

The God of Israel can be trusted. He is faithful. He is in control. He is able to help us in our time of need. You can put your faith in him.

Such a faith enables us to let go of our stubborn pride and see that God's way is always the best way. Faith accepts the healing to be found in the simple waters of baptism, and in God's Word, and in worship and prayer. God is at work through these simple things to bestow his grace and favor.

And when you have such a humble faith, you are able to finally rest safe and secure in God's hands. You can commit your life to the Lord with an unwavering trust and confidence. You can rest safely in his love and trust in his almighty power. If there is a problem, you take it to the Lord.

Like that young girl from Israel who was taken away to serve in Naaman's household, we can also live by faith. No matter what dire circumstances we may be facing, our faith can be strong and alive.

And, like that girl, we can point others to God of Israel who heals and saves sinners. We can reach out to people who are trapped and stuck and say, "There is hope! There is a God who loves you and who cares."

We can share our faith and reach out with God's love and compassion to all people. We can invite others to come down and join us, as we wash ourselves in the dirty waters of the Jordan River.

Come and be cleansed by God's love in Christ. Come, be born again and receive God's gift of healing and renewal in Christ. Amen!

SOME BAD NEWS AND SOME GOOD NEWS:
Mark 1:21-28

A wife went with her husband to the doctor. The husband had been sick for a while and the doctor had run a bunch of tests to find out what was wrong. The doctor takes the wife aside and says, "I've got some good news and I've got some bad news."

The doctor says, "The bad news is that your husband is very ill. He may die. But the good news is that if you do the following he may recover.

"What you need to do is to keep your house spotless; you have to clean it from top to bottom every day. This includes the kitchen and all the bathrooms. No germs at all. You also have to feed him three special meals a day. This special diet will involve lots of extra work and preparation. Also, don't burden your husband with any household chores or work. Don't let him do anything at all."

And so, on the way home in the car, the husband asked his wife what the doctor had said to her. She replied, "He said you're going to die."

This clearly was a case of bad news for the husband. We all know the difference between bad news and good news. The Bible also speaks of this difference. The Bible has a definite definition of what constitutes the good news of God.

Consider the following story. A few years back, a pastor was in the news because of a funeral he held at his church. He was preaching at the funeral of a long-time member, a lady who had passed away from cancer.

In the middle of the sermon, the pastor starts talking about how this lady had led a life of drunkenness and fornication. Therefore, she had most definitely gone to hell.

At this point, several people attending the service jumped up and started yelling at the pastor. A fight then broke out. The police had to be called to break-up the brawl.

Later, a church member defended her pastor. She told reporters, "He is duty-bound to preach the gospel, no matter what the circumstances."

Now, as far as I can tell, the problem here was that the gospel was not preached at all. That word "gospel," literally means, "good news." Someone being condemned to hell is not good news. Hell and damnation are bad news. This is a terrible prospect, the very opposite of the gospel.

What makes the gospel such good news is that it counteracts the bad news. When the doctor announces that the diagnosis has changed and the patient will live - that's good news. When a death row inmate receives a last minute pardon from the governor - that's good news. The good news always counteracts the bad.

Now, this doesn't mean that the bad news doesn't exist - it does. We do not deny the reality of hell and damnation. We do not deny the reality of sin and its devastating consequences. There is a time when we need to hear the bad news and acknowledge that it's true.

We need to acknowledge the problem of sin and its deadly effects. "If we claim to be without sin, we deceive ourselves and the truth is not in us." Anyone who is unclear about what sin is will be unclear about what the gospel is. You have to understand the bad news before you can comprehend the good.

"Sin" can be defined as rebelling against God and his ways for us. Sin is rejecting the Creator who made us. It is a turning away from the only source of life. That's why such a rebellion has such deadly consequences.

Paul says, "The wages of sin is death." Sin is a killer. That's the bad news. That's the reality we face. We are lost and dead. We have no hope of saving ourselves. "As for you, you were dead in your transgressions and sins."

What we need now is some good news. What we need is the gospel. Paul says, "I am not ashamed of the gospel because it is the very power of God for the salvation of everyone who believes."

The good news announces that God himself has come to rescue us from sin, death and hell. God comes to save those who were lost; he comes to rescue those who were perishing. This is the gospel and it is totally God's doing.

The gospel is about God's grace. It's about God's gift and God's Son. It's all about Jesus and what he has done for us. Paul says, "The wages of sin is death, but the gift of God is eternal life in Jesus Christ, our Lord."

God's gift - that's what the good news is all about. It describes what God has done for us in Jesus. And we see this work of Christ so clearly portrayed in today's reading.

Jesus goes into a synagogue and begins to teach. The people were amazed at his teaching because he taught them as one who had real authority, and not as the scribes (who quoted other teachers as their source of authority).

When Jesus speaks, the people take notice. He speaks with the authority of God. "You have heard that it was said to you of old, but I say unto you today."

When Jesus speaks, he speaks as the very Son of God. This is God in the flesh who was teaching in the synagogue that day.

But not everyone understands this. The people in the synagogue really don't have a clue about who Jesus really is. They know that there is something special and unique about him, but they just can't put their finger on it.

There is one person who immediately recognizes our Lord's true identity, a man possessed by an evil spirit. This demon-possessed man jumps up and starts yelling, "What do you want with us, Jesus of Nazareth? Have you come to destroy us? I know who you are! You are the Holy One of God!"

But Jesus puts a quick stop to all of this shouting. He commands the evil spirit, "Be silent and come out of him!" The Lord of all creation speaks his Word with power and authority, and the evil spirit has to obey. He immediately comes out of the man with a loud shriek.

Here, we see the Redeemer at work. He has come to do battle with the powers of darkness that enslave us. He has come to set us free from the bondage of sin, death and hell. The

Lord comes to undo all the negative effects of the fall.

As this evil spirit quickly realized - this Jesus of Nazareth is more than just a great teacher. He is more than just a Galilean peasant or a carpenter from Nazareth. This is the Holy One of God.

Jesus is true God, the Son who is begotten from the Father from all eternity. And yet, he is also true man, born of the virgin Mary. He is true God and man in one person.

And Christ comes into this world to preach and teach with authority. He comes to heal the sick and to cast out demons. He raises the dead, he feeds the hungry, he forgives sinners, he cleanses lepers, he restores the brokenhearted, and he gives himself to die on a cross. He does everything necessary for our salvation.

In Jesus Christ, we see how the Holy One of God humbles himself. He becomes our servant. He fully enters our life. He fully experiences what we go through. He becomes just like us, real flesh and blood, born of the virgin Mary.

Here is some good news for a world filled with bad news. Here is the gospel those who are hurting and in pain. Here is the Son of God who loves you with an everlasting love.

This is the compassionate Savior who reaches out to you today and who says, "Listen! I have some good news for you. Your sins are forgiven! I wash you clean with my holy and precious blood. I rescue you with my suffering and death. I defeat the devil and I have broken his power. You now belong to me. You are safe in my love."

This is the sweet gospel and it brings true comfort and peace to troubled hearts. This is the good news about a Savior who took our place and suffered our punishment. He experienced hell and damnation in our place. The Holy of God became the Sinner of God as he died on the cross. He carried our guilt upon himself.

"God made him who had no sin to be sin for us."

"Christ redeemed us from the curse of the law by becoming a curse for us."

"He was pierced for our transgression. He was crushed for our iniquities. The punishment that brought us peace was upon him. By his wounds, we are healed."

Through our Lord's suffering and death, we are set free from hell and damnation. We are set free from the bad news. We now enter God's kingdom of grace.

When the English scientist Isaac Newton was dying, he said something remarkable. He lay on his deathbed and was close to the end. His work was done and he thought about his life.

Newton finally said, "I have learned two great facts. One is that I am a great sinner. Secondly, Jesus Christ is an even greater Savior."

Today, we confess the very same thing. We confess that we are sinners (that's the bad news). But also confess that our Savior is greater than our sin (that's the good news). He has redeemed us. He has saved us, so that we might be his own and live under him in his kingdom.

This is our hope and comfort. This is the good news of the gospel. This is what we need to hear each day - God's message of love and forgiveness in Christ.

This message truly comforts our troubled hearts. It gives real joy and lasting peace. It bestows comfort and hope. It bestows God's gift upon us.

We now joyfully hear the wonderful news that the heavenly Father has welcomed us back into his kingdom. We are rescued and restored to the God who created us. This is good news indeed! Amen!

PERMANENT WAVE: Luke 24:1-12

A man was driving along the highway one day when, all of sudden, the Easter bunny ran right across the middle of the road. The man swerved to avoid hitting him, but the Easter bunny still got run over. The man got out of his car and was so upset, he started to cry.

A woman driving down the road saw the man crying and so she stopped. "What's wrong?" she said. "I just ran over the Easter bunny." She then told the man not to worry. "I know exactly what to do."

So, she goes over to her car and comes back with a spray can. She goes over to the dead bunny and sprays the entire contents of the can onto him.

All of sudden, the Easter bunny jumps up, alive and as good as new. He waves at the man and woman and then hops 20 yards down the road. He then stops, turns around and waves at them again. He does this several times until he finally faded from view.

The man was astonished and said to the woman, "What was in that spray can?" The woman gave him the can so he could read the label. It said, "Hair Spray. Brings dead hair back to life. Leaves permanent wave."

Today is Easter Sunday. This is a time to rejoice, laugh and sing. This is a day to celebrate and give thanks. Our Lord was dead but he has come back to life. And he now gives us a permanent wave of joy and gladness. The resurrection of Christ changes everything! It gives us a new outlook on what life is all about.

Today, we see how the women go to the tomb of Jesus. They have the spices they have prepared to complete the burial of Christ. On Friday afternoon, there wasn't time to do everything necessary. So, they come back after the Sabbath to finish the job.

When the women arrive at the tomb, they find that the stone has been rolled away. The tomb is open. They go inside and discover it is empty.

That's surprising because on Friday afternoon they had watched how Jesus was carefully placed in this exact tomb. But now, it's empty. Where is the body of Christ? What exactly has happened here?

All of a sudden, two angels appear inside the tomb. They are glowing with a dazzling brightness. The angels say, "Why do you seek the living among the dead? He is not here, but he has risen. Don't you remember how he told you that the Son of Man must be delivered into the hands of sinful men and be crucified, and on the third day rise?"

The women hear these words and they then remembered what Christ had said to them before. They now remember. These words of Christ give them a reference point for interpreting this strange turn of events. The Word of God explains the events of Good Friday. It all starts to make sense now.

And so, the women rush back to the apostles with this amazing news. "The tomb is empty! Christ has risen!" But the apostles do not believe their message. They are stuck in their unbelief. They think this is all nonsense. Dead people don't come back to life. If someone is crucified by the Romans, that's the end. The story is over. They are dead and gone.

And yet, Peter jumps up and runs to the tomb. He goes inside and looks around. Sure enough, the tomb is empty. Only the strips of linen used to wrap up the body of Christ are there. Peter departs at a loss of what to make of all of this. He is left wondering what's going on.

Notice how, at first, the empty tomb is a total mystery. Without the explanation of the angels, it just makes no sense. The empty tomb is a puzzle. Even Peter is left wondering what's going on. But that's how it is, isn't it?

Life is a mystery. What in the world is going on, anyway? Sometimes, you just can't figure things out. Life makes no sense. Why do bad things happen to me and my loved ones? Why is my life so hard and difficult sometimes?

This is where the words of Christ can help us make some sense of it all. Notice again how the angels directly quote the words of Christ. "Don't you remember how he told you back in Galilee that he must be delivered up and be crucified and on the third day rise from the dead?"

"Don't you remember?" the angels say. Don't you remember how he told you before it all happened? He told you plainly that he had to die for our sins. He had to be rejected and betrayed and condemned and crucified. He had to pay the price for our sins. He had to die for us, and then, be buried in that tomb.

But guess what? The tomb is now empty. He is not here because he has risen. That changes everything. We now have the key. Our life can now start to make sense if we put the cross and resurrection of Christ at the center of it. Faith will begin to understand.

On the other hand, unbelief thinks that all of this is nonsense. Unbelief fails to comprehend. It just doesn't get it. It thinks all of this talk about an empty tomb is crazy and useless. It's all foolishness and folly.

And I think that is the real tragedy of unbelief. If you don't believe in Christ as your

Savior, then you are missing out on so much. You are missing out on the joy of belonging to God. You miss out on the comfort of knowing that you are loved by God. You totally miss out on the fun of being a believer.

To know Christ is to know true joy and lasting peace. It is to know, beyond a shadow of a doubt, you are loved by a gracious God. Because he gave his Son for you, you now belong to him forever. What could be greater than that?

The words and promises of Christ always bring understanding. They are the key to interpreting everything. That message of the cross and resurrection of Jesus now frames our whole life. We now have a permanent wave of gladness and joy.

Again, this gladness and joy come only through the suffering, death and resurrection of God's Son. He had to suffer all these things. He had to go that way of the cross and empty tomb.

You see, without this message of the gospel, we are left wondering what's going on. Without the gospel, life remains a mystery, a riddle we can't figure out.

Without the gospel, confusion will cloud our existence. Fear and anxiety and unhappiness will fill our hearts. Worry will surround us like a dark fog.

But the good news of Jesus Christ brings enlightenment. Faith now begins to understand. We now have the key that unlocks the puzzle.

And really, when you get right down to it, the only thing that finally makes sense in this crazy world is, "He is not here; he has risen."

The resurrection makes all the pieces click into place. We can now see the big picture and understand God's plan and purpose for our life. Salvation in Christ is what it's all about. This salvation brings true joy and happiness. It puts a smile in on your face and a permanent wave in your heart.

Faith now trusts in God's Word and faith knows that all things are possible with God. Sins can be forgiven. The past can be erased. The dead can come back to life. Joy can fill our hearts. A permanent wave of gladness can shape our whole existence. We can make a new beginning!

Today is a day to celebrate God's love, mercy and grace. We know that Jesus died on the cross and that he was buried in the tomb. But that's not the end of the story.

But rather, it's just the beginning of something special, something more wonderful than we can ever imagine or expect. The journey has just begun. We are only getting started. The best is yet to come.

Just keep on living by faith. Keep on trusting that Christ has risen and the Risen Lord is with you each day. Have faith in Christ and rejoice in his blessings.

Experience the joy of Easter. Be glad, rejoice and sing! Let that permanent wave of faith fill your heart and soul, both now and forevermore. Amen!

THAT HEALING TOUCH:
Mark 1:29-39 & Isaiah 40:28-31

Today, Jesus is called to the bedside of Peter's mother-in-law. She has a high fever. That could be quite serious in those days.

So Peter asks Jesus to help his mother-in-law. Christ immediately goes to the woman, takes her by the hand and lifts her up. The fever left her and she was healed. Just like that!

Just like that, the Lord reached out with his healing touch. In fact, that evening the people of Capernaum brought all who were sick or oppressed by demons. The whole city gathered at the door of Peter's house. And Jesus healed many who were sick and he cast out many demons.

Try to imagine the scene. It must have been repeated so many times during our Lord's ministry. Jesus reaches out to people suffering from sickness and disease. He touches them with his healing hands.

Jesus touched the eyes of the blind and they could see. He touched the ears of the deaf and they could hear. He touched the tongue of the mute and they could speak. Our Lord laid his hands upon so many sick people and he helped them.

The same is true for us today. Our Lord reaches out to us and he touches us with the same healing power. And Christ not only heals our body, but he also heals our soul.

Our Lord touches our head with the waters of Holy Baptism and we are born-again. He touches our ears with the Word of God and faith is created. He touches our mouth with the bread and wine of Holy Communion and we receive his true body and blood.

Christ touches our conscience with the message that our sins are forgiven. He touches our hearts with the reassurance that he will never leave us or forsake us. Though his Word and Sacraments, Christ touches our sin-sick life and he makes us well.

On the cross, we see how the Son of God took our sin-sickness upon himself. The one who was perfectly healthy became sick. He carried that fever of sin which infects us all.

The doctor became sick. He suffered our disease. Isaiah says, "He carried our sorrows and the punishment that brought us peace was upon him. By his wounds, we are healed."

On the cross, Jesus paid the price for our sins. He was our substitute. He suffered that punishment of hell and damnation which we deserve. The Son of God was forsaken by the Father for three dark hours.

Our Good Physician took our place. He became sick so that we might be cured. By his wounds, we are healed. Jesus says, "It is not the healthy who need a doctor, but the sick."

Today, we hear Isaiah speak of another way that the Lord reaches out to us with his healing touch. Isaiah says, "Have you not known? Have you not heard? The Lord is the everlasting God, the Creator of the ends of the earth. He does not faint or grow weary; his understanding is unsearchable."

"God gives power to the faint and to him who has no might, he increases strength. Those who wait for the Lord shall renew their strength; they shall mount up with wings like eagles; they shall run and not be weary; they shall walk and not faint."

As we all know, there are times in our life when our strength is exhausted. We become emotionally and spiritually drained. We just can't go another step. We reach the limit to what we can endure. It just all becomes too much.

Isaiah speaks several times of those who are faint and weary. They fall exhausted to the ground. They collapse. That's you and me Isaiah is talking about.

We often are overcome by dire circumstances in our life. A death in the family, a fight with our spouse, a medical procedure, a conflict with a coworker, having problems with your kids, struggling with finances, trying to overcome that depressed feeling – on and on it goes. We all face stress and pressure, day in and day out.

Sometimes it reaches the point where we feel like we are running on empty. We are out of gas and are spiritually exhausted and ready to collapse. We just can't go another step.

But then, we hear Isaiah say, "The Lord is the everlasting God. He is the Creator of all things. God does not faint or grow weary. He gives his power to the faint, he increases our strength. Those who wait for the Lord shall renew their strength; they shall mount up with wings like eagles; they shall run and not grow weary."

You see, the Lord reaches out us with that healing touch and we are spiritually renewed; our soul is restored; our strength returns. God gives us a power that is not our own. He gives us what we need.

We can learn to deal with the pain and hurts we carry. We can cope with grief and loss. We can move on. We can make it because God's power and presence are at work in our life.

Listen, God loves you! He cares about you! You are not alone. He will stand by you, and give you something to hang on to, even in your darkest moments.

The story is told of a little boy who was not only afraid of the dark, but he was also terribly frightened by thunderstorms. One night, a series of severe storms swept over his home. The wind was howling. Lightning was flashing across the sky. The thunder was booming so loud that the windowpanes would shake.

The boy cried out, "Mom! Come quickly! I'm scared!" The mother went to her child. She said to the trembling boy, "It's alright. Remember, God is here with you."

The boy said, "I know God is with me. But sometimes I need a God with flesh and blood to hold me."

"A God with flesh and blood." That's what we have in Jesus. He is the one who comes to us in our hour of need, and he wraps his arms around us, and he says, "Don't be afraid! You are mine! I will never leave you or forsake you."

A lot of times in our life, we are like that frightened boy. The problems and troubles that surround us are so scary. We feel overwhelmed. But then, the God who has flesh and blood comes to us.

The Son of God reaches out and lifts us up with his healing touch. He lays his healing and helping hands upon us and we receive strength, courage and hope. We discover that we are safe. We can go on.

One final point: after we receive that healing touch from Christ, we discover that we can now reach out to other people. That's the wonderful thing about this gift we receive from God, we can share it with others. We can share the love and compassion of Christ. We can help others who are hurting and in pain. We can become the hands of Christ reaching out to others.

You can touch others with the love of Christ. You can visit that person in the hospital or nursing home. You share a word of encouragement and hope with them.

You can help someone who is overcome by grief and sorrow. You can share their tears and sadness. You can wrap your arms around them. You can lift-up their hearts with your prayers.

You can help a friend who is overwhelmed by the pressure of caring for someone sick or dying. You can help them out in some practical way and help them carry that weight. You can touch the conscience of someone who is burdened by guilt. You can say, "The Lord Jesus Christ forgives you. Your sins are taken away."

You can touch the lives of so many people, in so many different ways. And it is often that quiet, small thing you do that strikes the deepest chord.

Just like when Jesus healed Peter's mother-in-law. He simply went and took her by the hand, lifted her up, and the fever left her. Nothing fancy, nothing complicated.

So, too, we often touch someone's life through our simplest actions. That's how it is in God's kingdom. We simply live out our faith in the best way we can. We strive to faithful followers of the Lord. We are his people, his servants. We now become his hands as we share his healing touch with others. Amen!

THE KEY IS LOVE: 1 Samuel 3:1-10

There once was a Tennessee couple who had been married for over 70 years. Old Zeke was 94 years old, and his wife, Mae, was 92. Now Zeke was nearly deaf; his wife was also losing her hearing.

One hot summer afternoon, they sat on the front porch in their rocking chairs. Mae looked over at her husband with admiration in her eyes and said, "Zeke, I'm proud of you."

Zeke looked around and said, "What's that, Mae?" She again said, "I'm proud of you." "What? I can't hear you." Mae raised her voice and yelled out, "I'm proud of you!" Old Zeke looked away from her and said, "I'm tired of you too, Mae."

What we have here is a failure to communicate. This is a failure to listen. It's no accident that God created us with two ears and one mouth. We should listen twice as much as we speak. We need to listen carefully when someone speaks to us.

Today, we see the story of a young man who learned to listen. The young boy Samuel had been dedicated to the Lord's service at the tabernacle by his grateful mother, Hannah.

Hannah had prayed to God for a son and God had answered her prayer. So, Hannah dedicated her young boy to serve God at the tabernacle of Israel. Samuel would grow up under the guidance of Eli the priest.

In time, Samuel would grow up to be a great prophet, priest and teacher of God's Word. He would lead the people of Israel.

Today, we see how it all started. One night, when Eli and Samuel were sleeping in the tabernacle, the Lord called Samuel.

At first, he thought Eli was calling him. He runs over and wakes the old priest up. "Here I am. You called me." Eli said, "No, I wasn't calling you. Go back to sleep." This happened a couple of times.

Finally, Eli realized what was happening. God was calling Samuel. He then tells the young boy to listen, and the next time God calls, he should say, "Speak, Lord, your servant is listening." "Speak, Lord. I'm all ears!"

That's exactly what we need to learn to say. Like Samuel, we need to listen to God when he calls to us. When God speaks to us, we should also say, "Speak, Lord. I'm all ears! I'm listening."

God speaks to us through his Word, the Holy Bible. That's why we should read the Bible every day. We should read it, learn it, study it, and think about what it says. We need to open our ears (and our hearts) to what God says to us through his Word. God speaks clearly and directly through the Bible.

The Apostle Paul says:

+ "The gospel is the power of God for the salvation of everyone who believes."

+ "Faith comes from hearing the message and the message is heard through the word of Christ."

+ "All Scripture is God-breathed and is useful for teaching."

+ "The Holy Scriptures are able to make you wise for salvation through faith in Christ."

+ "Take up the sword of the Spirit, which is the word of God."

Our Lord Jesus says:

+ "My words are Spirit and they are life."

+ "Everyone who hears my word and believes what I say has eternal life."

+ "Blessed are those who hear the word of God and obey it."

+ "Father, sanctify them by your truth, your word is truth."

+ "The Scripture cannot be broken."

+ "These are the Scriptures that testify about me."

+ "Whoever belongs to God hears what God says."

+ "It is written, 'Man does not live by bread alone, but by every word that comes from the mouth of God.'"

+ "Whoever hears these words of mine and puts them into practice is like a wise man who built his house on the rock."

+ "For this reason I was born, and for this I have come into the world, to testify to the truth. Everyone on the side of truth listens to me."

+ "Heaven and earth will pass away, but my words will never pass away."

+ "Whoever has ears to hear, let them hear!"

We know this is what the Holy Scriptures declare and teach. We know we should be in the Word. We need to read the Bible everyday. However, the question is, "So, why don't we do it?"

Why do we have such a hard time reading the Scriptures? Why do we not read and study the Bible? I think there are several reasons.

Perhaps the most common reason I hear is that people say the Bible is too hard to understand. It's filled with difficult passages, and some parts are confusing. The Bible is just too hard.

Okay, while that may true for a few passages, let's not forget that most of the Bible is simple enough that even a child can easily understand it. Pretty much anyone can read the Bible and comprehend its message. That's the beauty of Scripture.

It's like a big lake in the mountains. It has shallow parts that child can safely play in, and it has deep parts that reach down to great depths.

The Bible has simple, straightforward stories that a young child can learn and easily memorize, and it has those passages you can study for an entire lifetime and never exhaust its meaning.

But we shouldn't let the difficulties throw us. There is an effective way to deal with those hard passages.

The famous preacher Charles Spurgeon once said, "For a long time I puzzled myself about the difficulties of Scripture. I would get stuck on one difficult verse. But finally, I came to the conclusion that reading the Bible was like eating a fish. When I run across a difficult passage, I lay it aside and call it a bone. Why should I choke on the bone, when there is so much nutritious food for me? Why should I stop eating the fish just because I encounter a bone?"

Let us be honest: the Bible is not that hard. Sure, there may some things we don't understand, but that's what Bible Study is for.

Bible Study is where we gather to study the Word together. We learn what it means and how to apply the message of God to our daily life. We learn how the clear and easy parts of the Bible explain the dark and difficult passages. Scripture interprets Scripture.

Don't forget the Bible is filled with stories of people just like us. These were real, historical people who faced the same problems and challenges we face.

For example, today we hear about Hannah, Eli and Samuel. These were people who encountered the same heartaches and sorrows we deal with each day. They faced the same problems and difficulties. And they were sinners, just like us. They made mistakes, just like we do. And yet, they all encountered a gracious God who spoke to their deepest needs through his powerful Word.

That Word delivers what it says - it delivers God's gift of forgiveness and life. It delivers God's gift of love. That's really what the Bible is all about.

God is love, and God loves you. God forgives you in Christ because he wants for you to live with him forever in the glory of a new heavens and earth. That's the basic message of the Bible.

And yet, we still don't hear this message of God's love. It falls on deaf ears and unresponsive hearts. We still don't read the Word. We don't listen to God's call. We fail to comprehend that message of God's love. Why is this?

Consider the following story. A young woman purchased a new book at a bookstore. She read a few chapters and then laid it aside. It really didn't interest her. In fact, she found the book quite boring.

Sometime later, she became acquainted with the author. A friendship sprang up. It developed into love, romance and a marriage proposal.

Now, the book was no longer dull. Every page became important. Every sentence had meaning. Every word was important and worth reading again and again. What was the difference? Love was the key.

Why do we find the Bible uninteresting and dull? Because we do not know the Author who wrote it. Why do we never read the Bible? Because we do not love the Author.

If we truly loved God, then we would love the Word he speaks. The key is love. God's love is the key that unlocks the Scriptures, and God has revealed his love to us through the cross and resurrection of his Son.

In Christ, we see the full extent of God's love for lost sinners. The Son of God gave himself for us on that cross. He died our death and suffered our punishment. He died and rose again for us.

+ "God has demonstrated his own love for in this - while we were still sinners, Christ died for us."

+ "This is love - not that we loved God, but that he loved us and sent his Son to be the atoning sacrifice for our sins."

+ "God so loved the world that he gave his Son to die for us on the cross."

This incredible love of God now touches our hearts, and we are changed. Our ears are opened. Our heart is renewed. We are born again, and we can now clearly hear the message of God's love in Christ.

The Risen Lord steps into our life and he calls to us through his Word. And just like young Samuel experienced, God calls us to his service and our spiritual journey begins. We experience God's love. We hear the Word and receive God's gift of life and salvation. In this way, faith is created.

Such a faith is an ongoing process. The Holy Spirit works each day now through the Word to establish and strengthen our faith.

You see, God himself helps us grow in his love. God the Holy Spirit helps us to read and understand the Holy Scriptures.

Through the work of the Holy Spirit, we learn to better know and love God. We learn to love the Lord who speaks to us through his Word. And we grow in faith and love each day.

The Bible now becomes interesting and fascinating. Every page becomes important, from Genesis to Revelation. The Word grabs hold of us and we are hooked. We want to read the Bible and study it every day.

Martin Luther once said, "The Bible is alive, it speaks to me. It has feet, it runs after me. It has hands, it lays hold of me."

Do you remember what Eli told young Samuel? He told him, "When God calls you, say, 'Speak, Lord, I'm all ears! Speak, Lord, your servant is listening.'"

That's the bottom line. Take some time every day to read the Bible. Make time to read God's Word. Listen to what the Lord is saying to you that day. Meditate upon his Word, and reflect upon what God is saying. Say, "Speak, Lord, your servant is listening."

And don't say that you are too busy or that you don't have the time. Don't say it's too hard to understand or that you find it dull and boring. Put away all your excuses and just pick up your Bible today and start to read it.

Open your heart to the power of God's love and you will be transformed. Little by little, day by day, week by week, month by month, you will be transformed into the image of Jesus Christ, the Son of God.

Such is the power of God's Word. Such is the power of the Holy Spirit. Such is the power of God's love.

God's love in Christ is the key that unlocks the Scriptures. God's love is the key to understanding, faith and salvation. It is the key that unlocks our entire life. Amen!

A SHORT SERMON: Mark 5:21-43

Today, we have a short sermon. No long, boring message. I'm just going to keep it short and simple today. There will be no stories or dumb jokes.

I'm not going to tell the story of how one day the big fence between heaven and hell broke down. St. Peter appeared at the broken section of the fence to inspect it. When he saw the devil walking over, he shouted, "Hey, Satan! How about getting your crew to fix this broken fence?"

The devil says, "We're busy over here. We can't fix your lousy fence." Peter answered, "If you don't, I'm going to file a lawsuit against you." The devil laughed, and said, "Oh yeah? And where are you going to find a lawyer?"

I'm also not going to mention how three guys on motorcycles pulled into a truck stop. Inside, there was only one customer, a truck driver quietly eating his dinner. He was a little guy, kind of meek looking.

The three bikers come over and start harassing him. One guy knocks his cap off, the other guy puts his cigarette out in his coffee, and the third one grabbed his plate of food and took it away.

The truck driver said nothing. He got up, paid for his dinner and left. One of the bikers, disappointed that they couldn't provoke a reaction from the little guy, commented to the waitress, "He wasn't much of a man, was he?"

The waitress replied, "No, I guess not." Then, looking out the window, she added, "I guess he's not much of a truck driver either. He just ran over three motorcycles."

Today, we skip such stories and jokes and go right to our reading. As we do so, we see how Jesus is surrounded by a great crowd that was following him. Our Lord was a source of hope to so many people, people who were desperate and in need of help.

One such person was Jairus, the father of a girl who was sick and dying. Jairus came to Jesus and said, "My little daughter is at the point of death. Can you come and lay your hands on her so that she may be made well and live?"

Christ immediately responds. He says, "Let's go!" And so, they start to work their way through the crowd. You know what that's like, trying to move through a big crowd of people all packed tightly together.

Now there was a woman in this crowd. She had a serious health problem, some kind of internal bleeding that wouldn't clear up. She was desperate, too.

She had heard about Jesus and how he had the power to help and heal the sick. And so she decides she's going to try to meet Jesus or at least try to reach out and touch him as he goes by. She said to herself, "If I touch even his garments, I will be made well."

Now, that's faith! Faith says, "Jesus has the power to help and heal. I'm going to reach out to him and trust he can help me in my situation."

This woman actually was able to touch the garments of Christ as he passed by and immediately she was healed. Jesus realized what had happened. He stops and addresses the people around him.

"Who touched me?" Jesus asks the crowd. The healed woman finally steps forward and confesses to Christ what she had done. And the Lord smiled and said, "Daughter, your faith has made you well! Go in peace and be healed of your disease."

But while Jesus was still speaking, some bad news came from the house of Jairus. His daughter had died. It was all over. She's dead. Gone forever.

Some people there even say, "Well, why bother the teacher anymore? Why bother? Jesus can't do anything now."

These people lack faith. They don't get it. You see, Jesus is more than just a teacher or great prophet. He is the very Son of God. He has the power to help and heal. He also has the power to give life to the dead.

But these people do not believe. They do not have faith. So they are willing to give up and quit. "Why bother any more? What can he do, anyway?"

But Christ says to Jairus, "Do not be afraid. All is not lost. Only believe! Have faith that I can help you." Then, the Lord says, "Let's go!"

When they get to the house of Jairus they confront a crowd of mourners carrying on. Jesus says, "Why are you making such a commotion? The child is not dead, but only sleeping." And the people laugh at him.

The Lord tells them, "All is not lost. I can still help." But the people laugh at Jesus. Again, we see the reaction of unbelief. People who lack faith laugh at the claims of Christ.

But Jesus immediately goes to where the dead girl is. He goes over to her, takes her hand and says, "Little girl, I say to you, arise!" And the girl sits up, alive! She then got up and walked around. Everyone is amazed. Jesus reaches out to this dead girl with his healing touch and she is made alive again.

But that's how it is: Christ is the healer and the giver of life. He is the Son of God who has the power to help and save, to deliver and rescue.

This is the compassionate Savior who cares about people who are hurting. He has great compassion for people who are facing a desperate situation. Jesus reaches out to people who are in great need, people like the woman who was bleeding and Jairus.

Listen, the Lord loves you and cares for you. He reaches out to you today in love and compassion. In fact, Christ loves you so much he was willing to lay aside his divine power and glory.

The Son of God humbled himself and made himself to be nothing. He was willing to go the cross to pay the price for our sins. He bled (just like the woman who was bleeding) and he died (just like the daughter of Jairus). Here we see how the Son of God shared our mortal life. He bled; he died; he suffers for us.

But through his passion, we receive healing and help. We receive forgiveness, life and salvation. And when we reach out to Christ in faith, we discover that he has already reached out to us first. Jesus reaches out to us in mercy and he says, "I say to you, get up, arise! Receive my gift of life."

Faith knows that Christ has the power to heal, to save and to give life. And so, we continue to reach out to him, no matter what our circumstances may be. We don't give up. We don't quit.

We continue to live by faith each day because we know Jesus loves us and he cares. Christ has mercy and compassion for all people, including you and me and everyone else.

And today, the Lord says, "Do not be afraid! Only believe. Trust that I love you and I care for you. Go now, your faith has made you well. Go in peace and continue to live by faith each day!" Amen!

HOW TO DEAL WITH A CRISIS:
Romans 5:1-11

Today, we look at how to deal with a crisis. Perhaps, before we begin, we should define what we mean by a "crisis." A crisis is a sudden event that catches us off guard. It upsets the balance of life. It is a decisive, critical moment that calls for some kind of a response.

A crisis is when something suddenly happens to us and we ask, "What do I do now?" It is a pivotal moment that calls for some kind of decision. It is a turning point, for better or worse.

Usually, we think of a crisis as something bad and negative. Something goes wrong for us. Some event that is hurtful and destructive suddenly occurs.

This is something we can all identify with. That's how it is for all of us. We all experience hurt and pain and trauma. Things do go wrong for us on a regular basis. You can expect the unexpected to always happen.

The Bible teaches that such crises are a part of life; they are woven into the very fabric of existence. There is no way to avoid them.

Bad things do happen to us, and they happen because this is a fallen creation. Our world has been ruined by sin; it is broken, damaged, ruined and corrupted. The balance of life is permanently out-of-whack.

This all started when Adam and Eve rebelled against God. That was the original, primordial crisis. This rebellion brought suffering and death into God's perfect creation. That's when everything started to go wrong for us. And crises have been happening ever since.

So, what should we do when a crisis occurs in our life? How should we respond? How can we be prepared for these unexpected events? And how do we cope with the aftermath?

There is no doubt that sudden crisis can be difficult to handle. Every crisis is a pivotal moment in our life, for better or worse. It calls for some kind of response. We have to make some kind decision and act in some kind of way.

Our response can be either positive or negative. We can either move forward or fall back. We can respond positively in faith, or we react negatively in confusion and doubt.

In the end, this is a matter of faith. A crisis reveals whether truly believe in God or not. Our faith is tested. We can respond as a believer or we can act like an unbeliever. We can trust that God is in control and move forward or we can collapse under the weight of unbelief, uncertainty and doubt.

The Bible teaches that the trials and tribulations we experience are opportunities for spiritual growth. James says, "The testing of your faith develops perseverance, and perseverance must finish its work so that you may be mature and complete."

Paul says, "We rejoice in our sufferings because we know that suffering produces perseverance, and perseverance produces character, and character, hope. And hope does not disappoint us, because God has poured out his love into our hearts by the Holy Spirit, whom he has given us."

In other words, for those who have faith that God is with them as they undergo a crisis, there is an opportunity for something positive to occur. We can grow stronger spiritually.

Paul says, "We know that in all things, God is able to work good for those who love him, who have been called according to his purpose."

The Bible does not gloss over the fact that suffering and trials take place in our life. The Bible is filled with stories of people facing a crisis. Think of Noah, Job, Abraham, Moses, David, Ruth, Esther, Elijah, Elisha, Jeremiah, Daniel, Jonah, Mary and Joseph, the Apostles and so many others.

But the Scriptures also teach that we have a basis for dealing with a crisis. We can live out our lives in the context of faith.

By faith, we are able to see that God is in control of all things and that God has a purpose and plan in everything that happens to us.

Through faith, we can see that, "In all things, God truly works for the ultimate good of those who love him, those who have been called according to his purpose."

Faith is the key here. Faith trusts God implicitly and is willing to follow God's ways. Faith knows that in everything that happens to us, in every crisis we face, God is able to bring something good out of it. And that is the good news for us today. That is the gospel. That is our hope.

Today, our Lord is calling us to a place of faith. He enters our life and issues that call that will change our life forever. Jesus says, "Come and follow me!"

Now, we face a decision. The Lord calls to us and we need to respond in some way. Christ says to all of us today, "The time has come. The pivotal point has been reached. The kingdom of God has arrived. The time is now for you to come and follow me."

Can you feel the sense of urgency in the Lord's call? Now is the time to have faith. Today is the day of salvation. The kingdom of God is here! Therefore, repent and believe the good news, and come and follow Christ.

My point is this: the time to believe in Christ is now. That's the only way you can effectively deal with a crisis. Now is the time to have faith and trust that God is in control of your life. Now is the time to repent and follow God's call for your life.

Whenever something bad happens to you, turn to Jesus Christ, the Son of God. He is your hope. He is the one who reaches to you in your moment of crisis and he says, "Take heart! Do not be afraid! But trust that I am with you in this moment. You are safe in my love. I will help you get through this. Together, we can make it!"

Our Lord calls out to us in our moment of crisis and he says, "Look to my cross and resurrection! There, you will find the strength and courage you need. There, you will see how much I love you."

When you look to the cross, you see how our Lord had his moment of crisis. The crisis came for him, and bad things happened to him. He suffered the ultimate trial and tribulation. He suffered the pain and agony of crucifixion. He carried upon his soul all the sin and evil of this entire fallen, broken creation.

The ultimate crisis occurred. All the bad things in the whole world were placed upon Jesus as he hung on the cross.

But God the Father was able to take all that suffering and work good out of it. God takes all the evil of the crucifixion and he works forgiveness. From death comes life, from suffering comes hope.

The resurrection of Jesus confirms our hope. The resurrection shows how God was in control all along. The Father had a purpose and plan in everything that happened. That was true for Jesus, and it's true for us as well. This is our hope.

Remember, Paul says, "Hope does not disappoint us, because God has poured out his love into our hearts by the Holy Spirit, whom he has given us." Our hope in Christ is confirmed by God's love, and "God has demonstrated his own love for in this – while we were still sinners, Christ died for us."

Listen, we know that in this life we have to face all kinds of unexpected events that can upset our balance. Life is filled with endless crises. Tragedy and heartache can happen to us at any time.

But remember how bad things happened to our Lord. He suffered all those things so that you might have hope, the hope of a new and better life, the hope of a new creation.

Because of Christ, you can deal with trouble and heartache. You can cope with any crisis that may come your way. You can respond with faith and fortitude. You can show perseverance and become stronger and more mature in your faith. As James says, "The testing of our faith develops perseverance."

The testing of our faith makes us stronger. It lifts up our eyes to see the day when there will be no more bad things, the day when God's new creation comes into existence.

And on that day, God will take away all the brokenness of this world and he will make everything new. On that day, a perfect balance will be restored and made permanent. All crises will be resolved forever in our favor. Then, there will be no more suffering and evil to deal with.

But the key is to keep on living by faith. Keep on believing, and be strong in the Lord and in the strength of his might. Persevere in your faith. Don't give up. Never surrender. Keep the faith and be strong.

The time is now to hear the voice of Jesus calling to you. He says, "Come on, follow me!

Come and experience my help and blessing. Come and journey with me on this trip we are taking together. I will be with you, and I will help you deal with any crisis you have to face."

The time is now for you to believe in Christ. Today is the day of salvation. Now is the time of God's favor.

"The time is fulfilled and the kingdom of God is at hand. Therefore, repent and believe in the gospel." Amen!

SALT IS GOOD! Mark 9:42-50

Salt has long been associated with many traditions in lots of different cultures. It has been linked to all kinds of old customs and beliefs.

For example, the accidental spilling of salt has always been considered bad luck. You never spill salt. Usually, throwing a pinch of salt over the left shoulder will nullify that bad luck.

An old Norwegian tradition says that spilled salt indicates the shedding of tears. Tears are salty, and they say you will shed as many tears as necessary to dissolve the spilled salt.

Salt is also associated with friendship because of its lasting quality. In the Middle Ages, salt was always presented to a guest first, before dinner was served. This signified hospitality and friendship.

In Hungary, it was an old custom to sprinkle the threshold of a new house with salt. This would provide good luck for the family moving in.

In some parts of Europe, a new-born baby would be sprinkled lightly with salt. This was thought to offer protection from harm.

Salt also symbolizes hard work because sweat and perspiration are salty. We will call someone "an old salt" if they have years of experience and hard work under their belt.

Our language is filled with all kinds of expressions that indicate the special role that salt has played. We say, "If you want to catch a bird, put salt on its tail," or "I'll take that with a grain of salt," or "That guy is the salt of the earth," or "He's so lazy. He's not worth his salt."

Today, we hear our Lord Jesus Christ speak about salt. Jesus says, "Everyone will be salted with fire. Salt is good, but if the salt has lost its saltiness, how will you make it salty again? Have salt in yourselves, and be at peace with one another."

In the Bible, salt was most commonly used with the sacrifices offered at the temple. All of the sacrifices were required to be seasoned with salt before they were offered-up to God. This was especially true for the burnt-offering which was offered up by fire to atone for sin.

Salt was also used to ratify covenants and treaties. Salt here symbolized fidelity, commitment, and truthfulness to your word.

Salt also stands for wise conversation. "Let your words be seasoned with salt," Paul told the Colossians.

And now, we hear Jesus say, "Salt is good. Have salt in yourselves."

Here, salt stands for the saving work of Christ; it symbolizes the gospel itself. We are salted with the cross and resurrection of our Lord. And this salt of Christ now empowers us to wisely serve others and live out our faith.

Salt is good because in our Lord's hands it has a purifying, cleansing effect. We are sprinkled with salt; we are purified and made clean. As Jesus says, we are salted with fire.

This is true because Christ himself was salted with fire. He is the final and perfect sacrifice, our ultimate burnt-offering. He was offered up to take away our sin and guilt. Our Lord has salted us with his own blood, sweat and tears.

On the cross, Christ sheds his blood. He experiences that unquenchable fire as he suffers the punishment we deserve. He experiences the fires of hell. He is forsaken and abandoned. He is cursed and damned. He sweats and does that impossibly hard work of suffering for the sins of all people.

That bitter salt was spilled as Christ sacrifices himself for us. His bitter tears were shed as he bears our burden. He is burned up with the unquenchable fire of hell.

At the end of his suffering, Jesus cries out, "I thirst," and he receives a brief refreshing drink. Then, he cries out, "It is finished!" and he says, "Father, into your hands I commit my spirit." He then breathes his last breath.

His redeeming work is done. It is finished. Sin has been atoned for. The price has been paid. We are now forgiven because of our Lord's salty sacrifice. We are now sprinkled with the blood of Christ.

Jesus says, "Everyone will be salted with fire. Salt is good. Have salt in yourselves, and be at peace with one another."

Salt is good! It is good to receive God's gift of salvation. It is good to hear Christ say, "I love you and I forgive you all of your sins." It is good to be forgiven by Christ!

That forgiveness now empowers us to serve others. We are salted to give of ourselves and to serve other people. This means we are now called to witness to others about the saving work of Christ.

We are missionaries who bear witness to Christ. We declare to others, "This is the Son of God! He died and rose again for you. There is hope in Jesus. There is salvation. There is someone who loves you with an everlasting love."

We tell others about our Savior. We reach out with the good news of what Christ has done for us. He rescues us from the fires of hell and brings us into his kingdom of grace. The Lord delivers us so that we can now be his people. We are his ambassadors.

And we are not only missionaries of the Word, but we are also missionaries of mercy. We care for others who are hurting. We seek to help others. We show mercy, comfort and compassion. This means helping others and serving them.

In a practical way, we are called to show mercy wherever God has placed us in our life. We show mercy within the context of our families, marriages and households. We show the love of Christ in our workplace and in our local communities. We become active and involved in our neighborhoods to help people going through hardship and difficulties.

We reach out to the hungry, the poor, and the needy. We care for the sick and dying. We help our friends who are grieving the loss of a loved one. We visit the elderly and homebound. We pray for those who need God's help and blessing.

Our Lord says, "You are the salt of the earth. You are the light of the world. Let your light shine before others, that they may see your good deeds and praise your Father in heaven."

There are so many ways for you to love and serve others. There are so many ways for you to be the salt of the earth. You can be a shining light as you share with others that incredible peace of God which passes all understanding. Speak God's truth in love; be wise in your conversation.

By God's grace, you are an ambassador for Christ. You are called to be a servant of the Word and a missionary of mercy. "You are the salt of the earth." As the Lord says, "Salt is good! Have salt in yourselves, and be at peace with one another." Amen!

WOW! I AM BAPTIZED! Mark 1:1-13

Today, we will take a look at the power of Holy Baptism. We will look at the baptism of John, the baptism of Jesus and our own baptism. And, in the end, we will see how the cross and resurrection of our Lord ties them all together.

Today, we see how John the Baptist was sent by God to prepare the way for the coming of the Messiah. John came preaching a baptism of repentance for the forgiveness of sins.

John said, "After me, comes one who is more powerful than I. I am not worthy to bend down to untie his sandals. I have baptized you with water, but he will baptize you with the Holy Spirit."

John also told the people, "Repent! For the kingdom of God is at hand. Repent and be baptized for the forgiveness of sins. Get ready for the coming of the Messiah!"

And when all the people were being baptized in the Jordan River, Jesus suddenly appears. He wants to be baptized, too. But why was Jesus baptized by John?

Did Christ need to repent? Did he need to have his sins washed away? Did he need to be forgiven?

The answer is "No." There was no need for Jesus to repent. He was not a sinner. He was the Holy One of God. He was sinless and pure. Christ was perfect. He never sinned in any way.

So, what's going on here? Why is Jesus baptized? Here's the point: when you see Jesus standing in the muddy waters of the Jordan being baptized by John, you see how the Messiah completely identifies with his people.

The Savior aligns himself with sinners. He undergoes John's baptism of repentance to conform to all that was required of God's people. In other words, Christ takes his place with us. He stands side-by-side with us sinners. He publicly identifies himself with those he came to save. He stands shoulder-to-shoulder with us in the dirty waters of the Jordan River.

But that's not all. This baptism of Jesus points in the direction he must go. The Messiah must go the way of suffering and sacrifice. What is begun in this baptism by John in the Jordan River will be brought to completion in the crucifixion outside of Jerusalem.

If Jesus identifies with sinners in his baptism, then he completes this solidarity by dying the death of a sinner on the cross. He dies condemned and forsaken by the Father.

On Mt. Calvary, Christ suffered God's judgment against sin. The Messiah suffered hell and damnation in our place. He undergoes the baptism of dying on a cross.

In Romans 6, St. Paul brings out this connection between the cross and baptism. Paul says, "Do you not know that all of us who have been baptized in Christ, were baptized into his death? We were buried with him through baptism into death, in order that just as Christ was raised from the dead by the glory of the Father, we too may walk in newness of life."

Here we see how the power of baptism is the cross and resurrection of Jesus. Through baptism, we are united with him in his death and Easter resurrection.

Our old sinful self is crucified with him on the cross. Then, we are raised up through the resurrection of our Lord, so that we enter with him into the new life which God gives. "For you died, and your life is now hidden with Christ in God. Since you have been raised with Christ, set your hearts on things above."

The power of baptism is the atoning sacrifice of the Son of God and his glorious resurrection from the dead. Baptism connects you directly to Jesus and everything he did for you. It connects you to his cross and resurrection. You receive his baptism and his perfect life.

And remember, this is a continuous connection. It is present every day and it is constantly occurring. "Your life is now hidden with Christ in God."

And yet, somehow, we forgot all about God's gift of baptism. I mean, we don't really think much about our baptism, do we?

When was the last time you said, "Wow! I've been baptized!" When was the last time you said, "I'm a baptized child of God! I've been connected to Christ." When was the last time you really thought about your baptism?

My point is this: don't forget the power of baptism. You have been connected to Christ. You have been baptized by the Holy Spirit. You now belong to the heavenly Father. You are his child and are a part of God's kingdom forever.

This is a powerful gift of grace, a gift bestowed upon sinners who do not deserve such a wonderful blessing. Baptism is God's gift, God's work, God's miracle. It is not something we deserve or earn or merit.

A lot of times we think we have to deserve God's grace. We believe we have to perform and earn God's love and forgiveness. We think salvation is something we have to achieve. We have to be good enough to go to heaven.

I once heard a joke about a man who fell on hard times. His business was falling apart and facing bankruptcy. His wife was leaving him. He couldn't meet the mortgage payments, so the bank was about to foreclose.

One snowy day as he was driving to work, he hit a patch of black ice and his car ran off the road and hit a tree. As he crawled out of the wreckage, the man looked up to heaven and said, "Why me, Lord? Why me?"

And then, a booming voice came from heaven, and said, "Well, the truth is - I just don't like you!"

That's how we think - God rewards us if we are good and he likes us, and he punishes us if we are bad and he doesn't like us. But the point to remember is that none of us are good when we stand before God. We are not good or likable. We are not holy, sinless and pure. Only one person was ever without sin, and that was Jesus Christ, our Lord.

Christ was perfect and without sin, and yet, he still stands side-by-side with us. He completely identifies us in every way. And, in the end, he took the punishment we had earned; he died that death we deserve.

The truth is that we are all fallen sinners. Left to ourselves, we are totally lost and condemned. We are dead in our sins.

But now, we see how the cross and resurrection of Jesus ties everything together. It completely connects together the baptism of John, the baptism of Jesus and our own baptism. It ties together our whole life.

Listen, you are forgiven because of what Christ has done for you. Through baptism, you are connected to him forever. You are brought into God's kingdom and you are a beloved child of the heavenly Father. That is the power of baptism. That is God's gift to you.

So then, remember this precious gift every day. Remember your baptism! Treasure this powerful gift and hang on to it tightly.

Start every morning by saying, "Wow! I'm a baptized child of God. I belong to the Lord forever!" (And shout it out with joy!)

You are now set free to live out your baptismal calling. You can put your faith into action. You can live for God. You can love and serve others. And you can walk in the newness of life baptism gives every day.

And there's another thing about baptism you should always remember. When you were baptized, God made a specific promise to you. He promised that he would never leave you or forsake you. He promised to watch over you for all of your life.

It doesn't matter if you are young and healthy, or if you are old and dying. Your life is surrounded by that powerful grace God bestowed upon you in Holy Baptism. It doesn't matter if you have Alzheimer's or dementia, God is at work in your soul, keeping you in the faith. You are a baptized child of God all the way.

Isaiah says, "But now, this is what the Lord says, he who created you, he who formed you, 'Fear not, for I have redeemed you; I have called you by name; you are mine. When you pass through the waters, I will be with you; and when you pass through the rivers, they will not sweep over you. When you walk through the fire, you will not be burned. I am with you!'"

That is the promise God made to you in Holy Baptism. That is the power of God's love in Christ. And that is your continuous connection to the Son of God's suffering, death and resurrection.

Wow! You are a baptized child of God! Go now and remember God's gift every day. Go now and experience his peace, receive his blessing and live in his love. Amen!

WE NEED TO PRAY: James 5:13-20

Today, we hear: "Elijah was a man with a nature like ours, and he prayed fervently that it might not rain, and for three years and six months, it did not rain on the earth. Then he prayed again, and heaven gave rain, and the earth bore its fruit."

Elijah was a great prophet and a man of God. He experienced many miracles in his life. Yet, when James talks about Elijah, he doesn't mention the spectacular feats or the great miracles of the prophet. He talks about his prayer life.

Elijah was known as a man who prayed. This is amazing. Even though Elijah worked many miracles, he did not take for granted that God wants us to pray. In fact, James says, "He prayed fervently."

Sometimes, we wonder, "Do I really need to pray? Since God is all powerful and all knowing, does my prayer really matter all that much? Isn't God going to do what he wants to do anyway?" Most people believe that. That's why most of us think we don't need to pray.

Why should I pray? Does prayer really change anything? Does my prayer actually matter? Why do I need to pray?

When we look at Elijah's life, we can begin to understand why we need to pray. Prayer has the power to change us.

Our text says: "Elijah prayed fervently that it might not rain, and for three years and six months, it did not rain on the earth. Then he prayed again, and heaven gave rain, and the earth bore its fruit."

This refers to the story in 1 Kings where Elijah confronted Ahab, the wicked king of Israel. Ahab had led the people of Israel into gross idolatry. They were unfaithful to the one true God who had saved them. And this all started when Jezebel encouraged her husband to set-up the worship of Baal, the god of the Sidonians.

Things got so bad that God announced judgment upon Ahab and the unfaithful Israelites. Elijah declared to King Ahab that a drought would come. He said, "As the Lord God of Israel lives, there will be neither dew nor rain in the next few years, except at my word."

Elijah then departed and stayed with a widow at Zarephath in Sidon. He stayed with her for about three and a half years. God then told Elijah, "Go and present yourself to Ahab, and I will send rain on the land."

Elijah then had the famous and dramatic confrontation with the prophets of Baal on Mount Carmel. After this, he declared to Ahab that it would now rain. Then, Elijah went to the top of Mount Carmel and he prayed for rain.

The first time Elijah prayed, nothing happened. The second time he prayed, nothing happened. This continued in the same way until the seventh time. Then, the sky grew black with dark clouds, the wind rose, and a heavy rain came pouring down upon the land.

Elijah prayed fervently and the rain came after the long drought. Can you imagine a drought lasting for over three years, especially in a dry place like the land of Palestine?

We know what damage a drought can do. Imagine a severe drought lasting for three years. Imagine everything just drying up and turning brown and dying.

I think that image of a severe drought can also be used to describe our spiritual life. Sometimes we go through a long period where it seems like our spiritual life just dries up and turns brown. It becomes dust and ashes.

We go through a drought of our soul. We stop praying, we don't worship, we don't read the Bible, we don't have faith. Like the Israelites of King Ahab's day, we fall away from the one true God who saved us and we become unfaithful.

But then, we are reminded of our Lord Jesus Christ. He is the One who enters into the drought of our parched spiritual life.

Our Lord comes to us, and he brings the sweet rain from heaven that gives new life. He bestows upon us the refreshing waters of Holy Baptism. He waters our soul with rain from heaven, the rain of forgiveness and grace, the rain of God's love and mercy.

This is true because our Lord entered our drought as he hung upon the cross. On the cross, Jesus carried all of our unfaithfulness and unbelief. He carried all of our sin and guilt.

Then, he cried out, "I thirst," as he suffers the punishment we deserve. He suffers our drought so that we might receive the rain from heaven.

This is the rain we pray for. We pray that God's would forgive us our sins. We pray that God would restore our souls and renew us with the sweet waters of his grace. And because God has promised to always answer this prayer, we are now able to approach him with confidence and certainty.

We are now able to pray because God has sent the rain of his love into our life. This changes everything. Love is the key. Now, prayer becomes not an exercise of trying to change God's mind, but an exercise of faith and acceptance.

First, we accept God's gift of grace in Christ. Then, we are able to accept God's will for our life. Then, we are able to pray with a humble and sincere faith, "Thy will be done."

"Elijah was a man with a nature like ours, and he prayed fervently." Elijah prayed in obedience to God's will. He did what God told him to do. That's what faith does. Faith obeys the Lord. Elijah also prayed fervently because he knew he needed God's help.

God says, "Call upon me in the day of trouble; I will deliver you, and you will honor me." God wants for us to turn to him in time of trouble. That's what Elijah did. He continually asked for God's help and deliverance.

Prayer is not meant to inform God of something he doesn't know about. Prayer is meant to remind us that we need God's help. Prayer is turning to the heavenly Father in a humble attitude which says, "May God's will be done in my life."

We pray, "Lord, I may not understand everything that is going on in my life, but I trust that you are in control. I trust that you are my loving and gracious heavenly Father. I believe that you always do what is best for me and my eternal salvation. Lord, I believe; help my unbelief."

James says that "Elijah was a man with a nature like ours." What this means is that Elijah faced the same challenges we all face. He experienced all the joys and sorrows we experience. He had great victories, yet, he also struggled with depression and defeat; he had great power from God, yet, he also experienced weakness.

Just imagine how Elijah must have felt during those long years of drought as he stayed with the widow of Zarephath in Sidon. That's a long time to live in isolation like that. (During that whole time, King Ahab was intently searching the whole region, looking for Elijah because he wanted to kill him.)

It would have been easy for Elijah to start blaming God for all of his troubles and woes. It would have been easy for Elijah to start complaining about his life and to find fault with God's ways. It would have been easy to give in to depression.

Yet, faith is able to raise itself above all these difficulties. Faith is able to pray with confidence and trust. Faith is able to say, "Our Father who art in heaven, hallowed be thy name; thy kingdom come; thy will be done on earth as it is in heaven."

This is true because God strengthens our soul with the power of his grace. God bestows his refreshing rain upon us and he waters our soul.

God puts his name upon us in Holy Baptism, and he claims us as his very own. And the heavenly Father says, "You now belong to me! I will never leave or forsake you."

Knowing all this enables us to pray in the right way. We can freely confess we need God's help. We can trust that the Lord will do what is best for us. We can submit to God's will for us, and we can know that any drought we may experience is only temporary. The rain will eventually come. Things will be green again.

But we need to pray. We need to pray because prayer strengthens our faith. Prayer enables us to share our burden with the Lord. Prayer lets us ask for God's help and healing.

Listen, you can always ask for God's comfort and strength. You can always ask for forgiveness and renewal. You can pray for the rains to come.

We need to pray because God wants us to. God wants for us to tell him what is really bothering us. God wants for us to share our burdens and heartaches with him.

With God, you can freely and openly share all of your failures and struggles. You can share your fears and worries. You can bear your soul before the Lord.

God understands what we are going through. That is why he invites us to come to him in prayer. "Come unto me, all you who are weary and burdened, and I will give you rest." "Call upon me in the day of trouble and I will deliver you." "Ask and it will be given to you; seek and you will find; knock and the door will be opened to you."

Martin Luther once said, "I don't pray because God needs it. I pray because I need it." We need to pray! Elijah was a man with a nature like ours and he prayed fervently.

Always pray to the Lord and ask for his help and blessing. Turn to God in faith today and receive once again the refreshing rains from heaven. Amen!

TO TELL THE TRUTH: Luke 4:14-30

Today, Jesus is in Galilee. He is teaching and preaching around Capernaum. The people all praised him for his wisdom and insight. His reputation began to spread throughout the region.

Then, Jesus returned to his hometown of Nazareth, where he had been raised as a child. As was his custom, Jesus went to the synagogue on the Sabbath, where he read these words from Isaiah: "The Spirit of the Lord is upon me, because he has anointed me to proclaim good news to the poor. He has sent me to proclaim liberty to the captives and recovering of sight to the blind, to set at liberty those who are oppressed, to proclaim the year of the Lord's favor."

Then, while everyone was watching him, Jesus sat down and said, "Today, this scripture has been fulfilled in your hearing." Now, that is an amazing statement! Absolutely incredible.

In essence, Jesus is announcing that he is the one Isaiah wrote about. He is that Anointed One sent by God. Right here, in Nazareth, the Messiah has come! "The Spirit of the Lord is upon me because he has anointed me to preach good news to the poor."

The people in the synagogue respond by saying, "What a minute! We've known you since you were a little kid. You went to High School right here in Nazareth. You're the son of that carpenter, Joseph. How can you be the Messiah?"

Jesus responds by saying, "Doubtless you will quote to me this proverb, 'Physician, heal thyself.' You will say, 'Do here in your hometown the miracles we heard you did at Capernaum.'"

Now, here comes the clincher. Jesus tells them, "No prophet is accepted in his hometown." And then he goes on to cite the examples of Elijah being sent by God to feed the widow in Sidon, and how Elisha was called by God to cleanse Naaman.

The people got so mad at this that they rose up and drove him out of the town. They took Jesus to the brow of the hill on which the town was built, so that they could throw him off the cliff.

The people got so angry they try to kill Jesus. They grab him and try to throw him off a cliff. But Luke says that Christ shook himself free and passed through the crowd and went on his way because his hour had not yet come.

Notice how Jesus tells the truth in the synagogue and the people get mad. He tells them the truth and they become enraged. Telling the truth can get you in big trouble.

That reminds me of the story of an elderly lady who came to church one Sunday morning. Nobody seemed to know her. The usher greeted her and asked where she would like to sit. She said, "I would like to sit right in the front pew, please."

The usher grimaced at that and said, "Ma'am, you don't want to do that." She said, "I don't?" He said, "No, you really don't. Our pastor is okay, but his sermons are really boring. To tell the truth, they are awful."

The woman then said, "Young man, do you know who I am? "No," said the usher. "I'm the pastor's mother!"

Telling the truth can get you into trouble. But today, Jesus tells the truth, the whole truth, and nothing but the truth. Our Lord says, "The Spirit of the Lord is upon me because he has anointed me to proclaim good news to the poor."

The Messiah proclaims good news and we certainly need to hear some good news today because we live in a world of bad news. It's all over the place.

It's hard to avoid hearing bad news. The news media constantly bombards us with stories of the foulness of human life. We hear of crimes and corruption, we hear of anger and hatred, of violence and shootings, of terrorism and bloodshed and the ugliness of life in today's world.

And we also experience bad news in our personal relationships. We experience endless family problems. We have trouble at work. We struggle to be a good parent. We fight with our spouse. We experience the death of loved ones. Our days are filled with endless sadness, grief and heartache.

But there is good news! God sends his Son to tell us the truth. And the Messiah declares that there is freedom for those oppressed by sin and evil. There is liberty for those who are trapped by the troubles of life. There is eyesight for the blind and hearing for the deaf.

Our problem is that we are deaf and blind to the truth that Jesus brings. We are unable to see the beauty and truth of the gospel. We are unable to hear God's call. And it seems like it's getting harder and harder for us to see the truth in this day and age.

The great advances in technology and computers and smart phones of the last few years provide us with a huge amount of information that constantly streams toward us. We now have easy access to a whole world of news stories. Each day, we have so much communication thrown at us constantly.

Overwhelmed with breaking news, strange and alarming headlines, click bait, and endless news alerts, we now tend to mistake raw data for truth.

Our attention span shortens and we don't even read past the first paragraph of any news story. And so, we end up collecting fragments and news-bites and headlines. We zip through and delete endless e-mails and spam. With all of this going on every day, it has become hard to get a handle on the big picture of life.

Simply put, we can't see the truth anymore. Our life has become fragmented and broken up. We are perplexed and overwhelmed by the quick pace of it all. We are mentally exhausted. It just becomes too much to process.

But God sends his Son to open our eyes and our ears. Christ comes to declare to us the beauty and truth of God's Word. He comes to show us what's really going in our life. The Messiah comes to tell the truth.

And the first truth our Lord proclaims is that we have lost our way. Plain and simple, we are selfish people who think only about ourselves. And you have to admit, the world of social media seems to feed this selfish desire. We all need to be "liked" and to be "followed." This is a very subtle seduction, one hard to resist.

And so, Jesus speaks about the truth of our condition. Because of our warped sense of self-love, we have not loved God as we should. We have not loved others. Simply put, we have failed to be the kind of people God wants us to be.

But Jesus also speaks the truth of God's grace. He says, "I am the way and the truth and the life." He says, "I give my life for you."

Christ says, "The Son of Man did not come to be served, but to serve, and to give his life as a ransom of many."

"Greater love has no one than this, that he lay down his life for his friends, and you are my friends."

"The Spirit of the Lord is upon me, because he has anointed me to proclaim good news to lost sinners. He has sent me to proclaim freedom and liberty to those held captive by sin and death. He has sent me to bring recovery of sight to those who are blind to God's truth and favor."

Listen, today this scripture is fulfilled in your hearing. Today, the Lord wipes away your tears and he lifts up your heart. Your eyes are now opened and your ears are attentive to God's Word.

The Messiah says, "Take heart! Do not be afraid! I am with you. Do not give up; I will help you. I will bless you with my favor and anoint you with my Spirit."

The Risen Christ continues to speak nothing but the truth to us. And he heals us of our brokenness and puts our life back together. He gives us strength to carry on. This truth of God is a real power.

His truth has the power to change us. It opens our mind and hearts to discover the real power of God's Word.

Jesus says, "If you hold to my teaching, you are really my disciples. Then, you will know the truth, and the truth will set you free." Knowing God's truth brings liberty and freedom.

What this means for us practically is that we now strive to live in God's truth. We will speak the truth to others. We resolve to put aside all falsehood and dishonesty. We stop telling lies. We are honest and keep our word. As Christians, we speak the truth in love.

Let's face it: we live in a very dishonest world, a world filled with lies and half-truths and rumors and allegations. Real honesty is a rare commodity. In today's world, who can you really trust?

This reminds me of the story of a little boy who was walking up and down on a beach one summer day. He wanted to go and swim in the ocean, but he had to do something first.

The boy saw a woman sitting under a beach-umbrella on the sand. He walked over to her and asked, "Are you a Christian?"

"Yes," she replied. "Do you read the Bible every day?" "Yes." "Do you pray?" She nodded her head.

Then the boy asked his final question, "Will you hold my wallet while I go swimming?"

If we are Christians, we will be truthful and honest. We will turn away from what is false and dishonest. We will be trustworthy people who do what is right and true.

Here, we follow the way of Jesus of Nazareth. He is God's truth made flesh. He says, "I am the truth." You can trust in him to help you to live in God's truth.

Therefore, let us hold on to his teaching. Let's show that we are his disciples by how we live out our faith each day. Then, "You will really know the truth and the truth will set you free." Amen!

DON'T WORRY SO MUCH:
Matthew 6:25-34

Did you hear the story about the man who told his friend, "I'm in big trouble. I have a mountain of credit card debt. I have lost my job. My car is being repossessed and my house is in foreclosure. But, do you know what? I am not worried about it at all."

His friend said, "You're not worried about it? How is that possible?" The man said, "I've hired a professional worrier. He does all my worrying for me. Now, I don't have to think about it."

"Why, that's fantastic! How much does your professional worrier charge?" "He charges $5,000 a year," the man replied. "But how are you going to get that kind of money?" his friend asked. The man calmly replied, "I don't know. That's his worry!"

Worry affects each and every one of us. If I were to ask how many of us are worried about something today, I wouldn't be surprised if all of us raised our hands.

There are certainly a lot of things we can worry about. We worry about our health. We worry about that latest pain that's been bothering us. We are afraid of going to the doctor because he may find something wrong with us. We worry about our spouses, our children, our grandchildren. We have family problems that keep us up at night.

We worry about the economy. We are fearful about the future and our financial security. We are afraid of losing our job or the company we work for downsizing. We worry about our country and the direction we are headed in. There are certainly a lot of things we can worry about nowadays.

Too much worrying can be dangerous for us. There's an old Russian folktale that describes the dangers of worry.

The story is told of how Death was walking toward a small village one morning. A man saw Death approaching and asked, "What are you going to do?" "I'm going to take 50 people today." "That's horrible!" the man said. "That's the way it is," Death said. "That's what I do." The man hurried to warn everyone he could about Death's plan.

As evening fell, he met Death again. "You told me you were going to take 50 people," the man said, "But over 100 people died!" "I kept my word," Death responded. "I only took 50 people. Worry took all the others."

This story reminds us that worry can have a negative impact on our health. It's been said that about 40% of all adults suffer health problems due to worry and stress, and about 50% of all visits to primary care physicians are stress-related disorders. And add to all that, those nights without sleep and you get a picture of the havoc worry plays in wrecking our quality of life.

But look at what Jesus says about worry in Matthew 6. He says, "Do not be anxious about your life, about what you will eat or what you will drink. Is not life more than food and the body more than clothing?"

Our Lord makes a bold statement here. In effect, Jesus says, "There's more to life than just worrying all the time. Why are you so anxious and afraid? Don't you have faith that God will take care of you and provide for all of your needs?"

You might say, "Look, I know Jesus says this, but that's impossible for me to do right now. You don't know what I'm going through in my life. Things are pretty bad. I'm really worried about my situation."

But again, our Lord says, "Why don't you just stop worrying about your life for a minute and take a look at the birds of the air. Consider the lilies of the field. Take a good look at God's creation. Can you see how the Father provides each day for the birds, the animals, the plants, and everything else? God is constantly at work, taking care of everything in this entire universe - don't you think that God will take care of you and help you in your hour of need?"

Do you see what Christ is doing here? He kind of shakes us by the shoulders and snaps us back to reality - God's reality. We sometimes get so wrapped up in our problems we lose sight of the big picture. We lose sight of God's kingdom. And when that happens, we can start to lose our faith.

Jesus says, "O you of little faith! Look at the birds of the air. They neither sow nor reap nor gather into barns, yet your heavenly Father feeds them. Consider again the lilies of the field, how they grow, they neither toil nor spin, yet not even Solomon in all his glory was dressed like one of these."

It's true. God feeds the birds and clothes the fields with flowers, and he will also feed and clothe us. It is our "little faith" that hinders us from seeing this reality. God is constantly at work in our world and in our life.

Jesus says, "Consider the lilies." Lilies grow from a deep root. The roots of a lily grow deep down in the soil to receive the nourishment it needs. In the same way, the roots of believers need to run deep into the spiritual nourishment God provides. Our roots should be going down deep into the rich soil of God's love in Christ.

Paul tells the Colossians, "Just as you received Christ Jesus as Lord, continue to live in him, rooted and built up in him, strengthened in the faith as you were taught, and overflowing with thankfulness."

That is the perfect antidote for worry and anxiety. Be rooted and built up in Christ. Remember the faith you were taught. Overflow with thankfulness to God. Continue to receive Christ Jesus as your Lord.

Our Lord says, "Do not be anxious. Do not worry so much and say, 'What shall we eat?' or 'What shall we drink?' or 'What shall we wear?' Your heavenly Father knows you need all these things. But seek first the kingdom of God and his righteousness, and all this will be added to you."

Notice again how Christ says, "Your heavenly Father knows what you need." You may think that you are all alone and no one understands what you are going through. But God knows. He knows exactly what you're facing in your life today. He understands your situation completely.

God knows what you need. He knows you need help and deliverance. He knows you need forgiveness and spiritual renewal. He knows you need his help. He knows you need Jesus.

That's why the Father sent his Son into our world. The Son of God becomes flesh and blood, just like us. He knew exactly what it was like to need food and drink, clothing and shelter. Jesus lived our life. He got hungry and thirsty; he was tired and exhausted. He had to sleep and eat, just like everyone else.

And he faced all the problems we face. In fact, he carries all of our burdens and troubles and heartaches. He carries all of our guilt and regrets, all of our sins and mistakes, all of our failures and defeats - and he takes all of that to the cross.

The Lord Jesus Christ dies for you on that cross. He puts to rest all of your deepest worries that you might enjoy his blessing and rest. "Come unto me, all you who are weary and burdened, and I will give you rest."

Our heavenly Father richly provides for us. He provides the cross and resurrection of his Son. He provides forgiveness, life and salvation. He provides baptism and Holy Communion and prayer. He gives to us everything we need so that we might be a part of his kingdom forever.

That's precisely why you can let go of all of your worrying about your life. God is in control! He knows what you need. Our heavenly Father will provide for you. You should trust in God's love and grace, especially when you face those hard times.

The apostle Peter says, "Humble yourselves, therefore, under God's mighty hand, so that he may lift you up in due time. Cast all your anxiety on him because he cares for you."

Peter says you can cast all your worries on God because he truly cares for you. God wants for you to hand over to him every single worry and concern you have. Give all your worries to God, and let him worry about it!

We can even say that God is our professional worrier (and the cost is totally free). All you have to do is give him your cares and concerns, and he will take care of them. Let God worry about it.

In this way, you can let go of the regrets of yesterday. You can discard all your fears about tomorrow. You can cast all your anxiety on God.

Yes, simply let them all go and let God take over. He can do your worrying for you. He can carry the load. He will deal with it. Let God take over your life. Commit yourself to him.

As Christ, our Lord says, "Do not worry about tomorrow, for tomorrow can worry about itself. Who of you by worrying can add a single hour to your life? Do not worry so much, but live by faith each day. Put God first in your life. Seek first his kingdom and all these things will be given to you as well." Amen!

REJOICE! 1 Corinthians 15:20-28

Today, we hear, "For as in Adam all die, so in Christ all will be made alive." This verse really sums up the whole meaning of Easter. There is life in Christ; there is a new creation that awaits us. There is hope, even in the midst of our sadness and tears. This is a message we all need to hear.

The truth is we often groan under the brokenness of life. We experience so many bad things. We are hurt and confused by the tragedies we face. Life is hard and difficult. Things are not what they should be. There is too much sickness and suffering, too much grief and heartache, too much death and dying. It's a tragic world we live in.

That's why we need to hear the Easter message. We need to hear some good news today. There's more to life than just what we see around us and experience each day. Eternal realities exist. A new creation awaits you! There is another life after this one.

That's what the women discovered when they went to the tomb on Easter morning. They went to the tomb with heavy hearts and tears in their eyes. They had just experienced the death of the one they loved. It was all so shocking and unexpected.

But God had a surprise waiting for them when they got there. The women were at first perplexed by the open tomb. However, they were even more surprised by the angels who suddenly appeared.

The angels had an amazing message. They said, "Why do you seek the living among the dead? He is not here; he has risen. Remember how he told you that the Son of Man must be delivered into the hands of sinful men, and be crucified, and on the third day rise."

Jesus Christ clearly taught and spoke about the necessity of his suffering and death. He repeatedly said, "The Son of Man must be delivered into the hands of sinful men and be crucified, and on the third day rise."

Our Lord knew what he had to do. He knew that he had to experience the passion in order to save this broken, dying world. He had to go to the cross. He had to suffer and die.

Jesus had to take upon himself all of the evil and brokenness of this entire world. That's what happened when our Lord was crucified. He was making all things new through his cross and resurrection.

Paul says, "In the same way that death entered this creation through one man, so also, the resurrection now comes through another man. For as in Adam all die, so also in Christ, all shall be made alive."

Notice how Paul refers to the story of Adam's fall. He basically says, "If you don't understand what happened in the fall of Adam, you're not going to understand what happened on Easter."

That's true. If you don't understand the fall, then you can't understand why Jesus had to go to the cross. If you don't understand how our sin and rebellion ruined a perfect creation, then you will never make sense of a world filled with tragedy and sorrow; you'll never understand why bad things happen.

The Bible says that death entered this world through the fall of Adam. That's when perfection became ruined. That is when suffering, tragedy and heartache came into existence. Just look at the story of Cain and Abel, the first children of Adam and Eve. Bad things happen because we sinned and lost a perfect world.

But if Adam brought death and brokenness, Christ brings life and healing. "For as in Adam all die, so also in Christ all shall be made alive."

You see, Christ makes all things new through his passion. Our Lord takes all the sin and guilt of Adam and Eve, Cain and Abel, and everyone else who has ever lived, upon himself. He carries all of our brokenness and heartache. In Christ, God himself enters into this fallen world.

God himself does what we could never do. God himself bears our burden. God himself dies on the cross. God makes all things new through the cross and resurrection of his Son. "God was reconciling the world to himself in Christ, not counting men's sins against them."

When you look at the story of the passion, you can see how it all leads to those three hours of darkness at the very end. A terrible darkness covers the land as the Son of God hangs on the cross and carries the sin and guilt of the entire human race. He is forsaken by the Father. He suffers our punishment. He bears our burden. But, at the end of it all, the darkness lifts, and Christ cries out, "It is finished!"

That is a cry of victory, a cry of vindication. All in now finished! Our sin has been dealt with. Our brokenness is now healed. Our death has been defeated. "For as in Adam all die, so also in Christ all shall be made alive."

Paul says that the sting of death has been decisively dealt with. Christ has been made alive and that resurrection is the victory of God which is ours by faith.

"Christ has indeed been raised from the dead, the first fruits of those who have fallen asleep." "Thanks be to God! He gives us the victory through our Lord Jesus Christ." "We are more than conquerors through him."

What this means is that the burial of Christ was only a temporary arrangement. Our Lord died, he was buried and the tomb was sealed up tight. But that was only a temporary situation.

And when you think about it, the same is true for us as well. We often forget that. Our death is only a temporary arrangement. There is another life after this one. There is the promise of the resurrection and a new creation to come.

There is more to life than just what we see around us today. Eternal realities await us. This is our faith; this is what we believe to be absolutely true. As we confess in the creed, "I believe in the resurrection of the dead and the life of the world to come."

This is true because of Christ. He does what we could never do. He defeats the power of death. He reverses the effects of the fall of Adam. He brings healing and hope and a brand new life. "For as in Adam all die, so also in Christ all shall be made alive."

Listen! Christ loves you and he doesn't want you to live in sadness and defeat. He wants for you to rejoice and be glad. He wants for you to realize that an eternity of joy and happiness awaits you.

You have the promise of a brand new life in a brand new resurrection body. All of this is waiting for you in the God's new creation.

Therefore, rejoice! Laugh and celebrate! Remember the powerful promises which the Lord makes to you through his cross and resurrection. Remember the meaning of Easter. Remember all that Christ has done for you.

Through faith in his promises, you are now able to cope with the tragedies and sorrows of life. Through faith in Christ, you can find renewed courage and hope.

Therefore, be strong in the Lord and in the strength of his might. Live every day in the power of our Lord's resurrection. Set your mind on things above and know that Christ is with you today.

Christ has risen! He has risen, indeed! Rejoice! Amen.

BLIND SPOTS: John 9:1-41

I don't know if you ever had this terrifying experience I'm about to mention. This will give you gray hairs. It will scare you to death. It will take a few years off your life. I'm talking, of course, about teaching your teenagers how to drive a car.

I remember teaching my daughters how to drive. They turned out to be good drivers, but along the way, I experienced a lot of tense moments of almost running over mailboxes, almost swerving into oncoming traffic, almost running through stop signs they didn't see. One daughter had the tendency to veer to the left while first driving. The other daughter would veer to the right.

And I remember I spent a lot of time talking about "blind spots." You know what a blind spot is. If you're driving in a car and are relying on your rear view mirrors to check the lanes behind you, there are some spots that you still won't be able to see.

You have blind spots on the right back and left back corners of your car. This means you have to turn your head and take a look over your shoulder before you change lanes.

Blind spots are created because we don't have eyes in the back of our heads. It is physically impossible to see everything at once. Today, we hear Jesus talk about blind spots.

Our Lord refers to the Pharisees as being blind. The irony is that Christ had just healed a man who was born blind. And in the aftermath of that miracle, the Pharisees tried to find a legal technicality to delegitimize what Jesus had done for this blind man

They said because Jesus healed on the Sabbath, this proved he was not sent by God. In their eyes, that made him a false Messiah. However, in all of this wrangling over keeping the Sabbath, they revealed they had a blind spot where Jesus was concerned.

Our Lord even said to them, "I have come so that those who do not see may see, and that those who think they see will realize they are blind." And revealing their arrogance and pride, the Pharisees responded to Jesus by saying, "What? Are we also blind?"

The truth was the Pharisees had spiritual blind spots - they couldn't see what God was doing in Christ. God had just performed a tremendous miracle through his Son, and still, these religious leaders couldn't see it. When you've got a spiritual blind spot, God may be doing something fantastic right before you, and you still can't see it.

This reminds me of the story of how Sherlock Holmes and Dr. Watson went on a camping trip. After a good meal and a bottle of wine, they lay down for the night and went to sleep.

Some hours later, Sherlock Holmes awoke and nudged his faithful partner. He said, "Watson, old boy, look up and tell me what you see." Watson replied, "I see millions and millions of stars." "And what does that tell you?" Holmes asked.

Watson pondered for a minute. "It tells me that there are millions of galaxies and potentially billions of stars. I also observe that Saturn is in Leo. Thus, I deduce that the time is approximately a quarter past three. Because there are no clouds tonight I suspect that we will have a beautiful day tomorrow. Why? What does it tell you?" Holmes said, "Watson, you idiot, someone has stolen our tent!"

Sometimes we are totally blind to what's going on right before us. We can be blind to what God is doing for us right now in our life.

How many times have you seen people who are unhappy because they are never satisfied? Although we live in such affluence and material comfort, we still complain.

We complain because our cable bill is getting higher. Our cell phones have roaming charges. Our new car isn't self-driving. Our restaurant no longer carries our favorite meal. Our spouse is not perfect. Our kids get an A- instead of an A+. On and on it goes.

We have blind spots all around us. We just can't see what great things God is doing right now in our life. And if we could see, we would jump for joy at how good God has been to us. We have food to eat, clothes to wear, a roof over our head, people to love, air to breathe, strength to live. Oh, praise the Lord!

The Pharisees should have been jumping for joy that a blind man could now see. They should have been glad that God has sent to us his Messiah to save us. But they had a spiritual blind spot when it came to Jesus.

Remember, these Pharisees were dedicated and committed religious leaders. They were well trained and respected in the community. They could discuss doctrine with the best of them. They were known for their spirituality and for their strict religious observance. Good church members, one and all.

We often chide the Pharisees for their hypocrisy, but you need to realize they were active church members. They were reading the Scriptures on a daily basis and strictly adhering to the religious law of their day.

But Jesus says that even if you are spiritually gifted, there still may be some blind spots. It doesn't matter who you are, it doesn't matter how many years you've been a church member, it doesn't matter how committed you are - everyone has a blind spot.

Listen: when you are driving a car, you had better be aware of the blind spots behind you. You had better look over your shoulder and check, before you change lanes or make any kind of move in traffic. The same thing holds true for us about our spiritual blind spots. We need to confess that we have them.

Our Lord says that there are basically two kinds of people - those who were blind and realize it, and those who think they can see but are actually blind. Notice that both of these groups are blind. But what makes all the difference is realizing your true state.

You have a blind spot, and so do I. We all are blind when you really get right down to it. The problem here, simply put, is that we are sinners.

We are sinners by nature. That makes us arrogant and self-centered people. We think that we are center of the universe. Everything revolves around us. We know it all, we are always right, we've got all the answers, we can never be wrong. We can see it all so clearly! Why can't everyone else see that?

However, when you admit you have a blind spot, you are ready for some spiritual healing. "If we say that we have no sin, we deceive ourselves and the truth is not in us. But if we confess our sins, God is faithful and just; he will forgive us our sins and cleanse us from all unrighteousness."

In other words, if we say we have no blind spots, we are not being honest with ourselves. We need to come clean and admit that we have been selfish and arrogant. We have failed to be the kind of people wants us to be. We have not lived in faith and love. We have taken God for granted. We have been blind.

The good news today is that the Light of the world has stepped into our lives. He has put mud on our eyes and he says, "Go, wash yourself in the waters of Holy Baptism. Go and remember how I died on the cross for all of your blindness. Go and let the light of God's love shine upon you once again. Then, you will clearly see."

Yes, the Son of God opens our eyes and we see him standing right before us. He heals our spiritual blindness and shines his light upon us. We now become children of light. We can see how God is constantly at work in our life.

We can clearly see how our Lord Jesus goes to the cross for us. He is that Servant of the Lord mentioned by Isaiah. He becomes blind in our place as he carries all of our sins. He bears our burden and suffers our punishment. He takes our blindness upon himself by dying on the cross.

Now, you can clearly see how much the Lord loves you. Look at everything Christ did for you – look at his passion, look at his suffering, look at his shed blood and his death. Look and see how much God loves you!

"God has demonstrated his own love for us in this: while we were still sinners, Christ died for us."

And there is something else we can now see. We now understand that God is always at work in our life. His love is constant and his presence is real. His mercy is unending. His power is constantly at work every day of our life.

We now perceive that everything we have is a gracious gift from our heavenly Father. Life is a gift. Health is a gift. Our family is a gift. Our possessions are a gift. Salvation is a gift. Everything is a gift from God. Can you see that?

Today, we look and see the glory of Christ. We experience the bright Light of the world shining upon us. He opens our hearts and eyes to see that he truly is the Messiah of Israel, the promised Servant of the Lord.

And Christ has come to make us children of God's light, people who follow what is right and true. Here, it is the Lord himself who is teaching us how to drive through this life. He keeps us from veering off the road. He keeps us on the road and reminds us to check our blind spots and to confess our sins.

The Lord God teaches us how to safely drive and how to receive his gift of forgiveness each day. He opens our eyes so that we can be thankful for all the blessings he so richly bestows on us. God is good and he is good all the time.

But most especially of all, God the Father reminds us how much he loves us. He continually leads us back to the cross and empty tomb of his Son. There, we find the strength and power we need to make it through the day.

Now we are able to safely drive through this life, until that day when we will drive through the gates of heaven and park our car forever in God's new creation. Amen!

YOU ARE FORGETTING SOMETHING:
Mark 6:45-56

To set the stage for today, last week we saw how the disciples had just come back from ministering to people who were hurting and in need. Jesus sent them out two by two, and he gave them his power and authority.

The disciples went forth preaching and teaching and sharing God's Word. They healed the sick and cast out demons. It was a busy missionary trip.

Then, after coming back, they gathered around the Lord for some quiet time and rest. But because Jesus was so popular at this time, great crowds surrounded him constantly. He and his disciples had no chance to rest for a while.

Seeing this, Jesus says, "Let's get into the boat and go away privately, to the other side of the lake." It was a good plan, but the people saw the direction they were going and decided to follow them on land around to the other side. They ran on foot and even arrived before them.

When Jesus and his disciples arrived in the boat, there were so many people waiting for him on the shore. The Lord looked at these people and he saw that they were like sheep that had no shepherd.

Christ was moved with compassion, and he began to teach them and to heal their sick. This went on all day long, into the afternoon. Finally, the day was almost over.

Since they were in a remote place with nothing to eat nearby, the disciples suggested that Jesus send the crowd away. But Christ had other plans.

First of all, notice how our Lord is moved with compassion at the sight of these people who are hurting and in need.

I don't know what your individual need might be today, but our Savior knows. He knows and he cares. It always touches his heart.

Whatever difficulty or heartache you are dealing with right now, it touches the heart of Christ. It could be a big need or it could be something little. It doesn't matter because you've got the Lord's attention today.

You might be dealing with:

- A serious health problem
- Growing older
- The death of a loved one
- A financial need
- Loneliness

- Depression
- A broken relationship
- A marriage problem
- Conflict in your family
- Having trouble with your kids
- An unsatisfying job
- Worry and anxiety
- A drug addiction
- Alcoholism
- An immoral lifestyle
- Being trapped in bad circumstances
- Having no hope for the future
- Feeling suicidal

It doesn't matter what your situation is. The Son of God is able to help you. There is nothing beyond his power. There is nothing too hard for him. There is nothing that he cannot fix. There is no life too broken that our Savior can't put back together again.

Christ is filled with compassion for people who are hurting and in trouble. That's why he decides that he is going to feed this hungry crowd.

Jesus tells his disciples to find out if anyone has any food. But all they come up with are five loaves and two fish. Jesus then prays to the Father and blesses the bread and fish, and then, he feeds over five thousand people.

What a tremendous miracle! What a display of our Lord's mighty power. From just a few loaves and fish, he produces a miracle so big that it feeds this great multitude and leaves twelve baskets full of leftovers.

The Lord meets their need and sends the people home with more than they asked for. Christ goes above and beyond what we could ever imagine.

Now, we are finally ready to look at today's reading. Remember, the disciples are still tired from their missionary journey. They still needed some rest.

What happens next is this: Jesus makes them get back into the boat and he sends them back to the other side. He will stay behind to send the crowds away.

After the crowds are gone, Jesus went up on a mountain to pray. The evening gave way to night. The weather quickly turned. A series of thunderstorms come roaring out of nowhere.

The disciples were now caught in the middle of the Sea of Galilee in an open boat. The storms are so fierce they thought they were going to capsize and drown. But Jesus came to them during the fourth watch of the night (around three o'clock in the morning).

At the darkest hour, the Lord came to them, walking on the water. When the disciples saw

Jesus walking on the water, they were terrified. They cried out in fear. They totally panicked.

But Jesus yelled out to them, "Take heart; it is I. Do not be afraid!" Then, Christ got into the boat and immediately the storm stopped. It was all over, just like that! The wind and waves ceased. The waters were again calm and quiet.

When the Lord steps into a situation, there are immediate results. Christ has the power to heal and help; he has the power to save and rescue. He can change your life and set you free. Just one touch of his garment is all you need today.

That is what the disciples eventually learned. But it took them a long while. Mark says the disciples were utterly astonished by what had just happened. This was something that deeply spooked them. And notice how Mark specifically says they were confused because "they did not understand about the loaves."

Think about that for a moment. "They did not understand about the loaves." In other words, they focused so much on the storm that they forgot all about the great miracle that Jesus had worked just a few hours earlier. They totally forgot about the miracle of the loaves and fish.

The disciples failed to appreciate the incredible power of the Son of God. They underestimated his love and compassion. They forgot who their Savior really was.

But that's how it is, right? When a crisis suddenly comes roaring out of nowhere, we forget all about Christ and his power. The storm comes and we panic and fall apart.

We feel overwhelmed. We think we are all alone and trapped. We feel hopeless and unable to cope anymore. The storm is crashing all around us and we think our boat is about to capsize and sink.

But listen, you're forgetting something. You're forgetting about the power of the Son of God. You are forgetting about the love and compassion of Christ. You're forgetting who your Savior is, and what he has already done for you.

Do not forget the power of God's love revealed through Jesus Christ. God's love is the key because that love is powerful and effective and it is able to help you in your time of need.

Never forget that it was around three o'clock on a dark Friday afternoon when our Lord came to us. At the darkest hour, we see Jesus hanging on a cross.

On that cross, he walked upon the stormy waters of our sins and he allowed himself to sink down into the very depths of hell. Christ suffered the terrible punishment we deserve. He took all of our darkest sins upon himself, and then he sunk down into the murky depths of hell and damnation.

That is the greatness of God's love – Christ gave himself for you. Here is a love that will not let go, a love that never gives up.

Christ has done for us far more than we can ask or think. Our Lord has met our greatest need. He freely bestows forgiveness, he conquers sin and death, he defeats the power of hell itself.

And now, Jesus says, "Take heart; it is I. Your sins are forgiven - completely, totally and absolutely. You are rescued and saved. I love you, and I am with you in this situation you are facing right now. Do not be afraid!"

Jesus now steps into the boat of our life, and we discover that all those storms and winds cease to overwhelm us. Suddenly, we discover that if we have Christ, we have all that we need. Everything is going to be alright. If Christ is with you in the boat, you are safe.

Christ has the power to still our troubled hearts. He can conquer all of our fears. He can quiet the stormy waters of our life. Just one touch of his garment is all that we need. A little faith goes a long way.

You need to say, "Lord, I know you have the power to help me. You can make all things new. Have mercy upon me! Help me in my hour of need!"

And don't forget about the loaves. Don't forget that if Christ is able to feed the hungry crowds, and if Christ is able to walk on the water and still the storm, and if Christ is able to die on the cross and rise from the dead, then he can certainly help you in your hour of need.

The Risen Lord can help you through the worst storm. He can give you strength to cope and the power to keep going. He restores hope and renews faith. Our Lord deals gently with those who are weak and faltering. "A bruised reed he will not break and a smoldering wick he will not snuff out."

And today, Jesus says, "Don't forget my heart is filled with compassion for you. Don't forget everything I have done for you. But always remember, you are safe in my love. You are mine, both now and forevermore!" Amen.

A BREATH OF FRESH AIR:
Acts 2:1-11 & Genesis 11:1-9

John Newton is the writer of the hymn "Amazing Grace." He was a British sailor involved in the African slave trade in the 1700's. He became a Christian in midlife and became a strong witness to God's amazing grace which totally changed his life.

A few weeks before he died, a friend was having breakfast with him. Their custom was to read from the Bible after the meal. Because John's eyes were growing dim, his friend would read and then John would make a brief comment on the passage.

On that day, the selection was from 1 Corinthians 15. When the words "By the grace of God, I am what I am" were read, John was silent for several minutes.

Then Newton said, "I once was an evil person doing despicable acts that I deeply regret. I lived in shame and disgrace, struggling daily with a guilty conscience. But then, I discovered the grace of God. I saw his undeserved love in the cross of his Son, Jesus. The Holy Spirit opened my eyes to see the power of Christ's atoning blood. I was blind, but now I see. I was lost, but now am found.

Yes, by the grace of God, I am what I am today."

That is the hope of every believer. "By the grace of God, I am what I am today." We know that through the grace of the Holy Spirit, we can change. We can be set free from old sinful ways. We can have a clean conscience and a clean heart.

That is the theme of Pentecost in Acts 2. The meaning of Pentecost is that God was doing something new here. God was sending a breath of fresh air. He was bringing in sweeping changes. He was undoing and breaking a curse that had been in effect for many generations.

Let's go back to Genesis 11 to understand the background. In Genesis 11, we have the story of the tower of Babel. After the flood, God told the sons of Noah to replenish the earth and fill it. Mankind was to go forth and repopulate the world.

But instead of following God's command, the people gathered in the plains of ancient Babylonia to build a city with a great tower. They used the latest technology for their building project. They used all their skill and prowess to oppose God.

They were arrogant and defiant, full of pride and boasting. They said, "Come, let's build ourselves a city with a great tower that will reach to the heavens, so that we might make name for ourselves, and not be scattered over the face of the whole earth."

"Let's make a name for ourselves," they said. "Let's build a huge city with a tower that reaches to the skies – a big, eternal monument to our greatness!" In essence, they wanted to be famous. They wanted applause and fame. They wanted to reach up and break through the gates of heaven. They wanted to be as great as God himself.

But their success rested on their common language. If they could work together, they could do anything. Even God was aware of this.

God looked down from heaven, and said, "I see that they have one language and they have a ton of pride, too. I need to put a stop to all this." So, he confused them. He gave them different languages, and they couldn't finish the building project. And God scattered them across the face of the earth.

Of course, the irony of it all was that they got a name for themselves after all. They wanted a famous name, but what they got was the infamous name of "Babel," which means, "confusion." They wanted be defy God's command, but that didn't work out too well. Despite their greatest efforts, they were scattered anyway.

This whole episode is a striking judgment on human sin. It is God responding to the arrogance and pride of people who wanted to be as great as he is.

It's the same old trick the devil used in the Garden of Eden. The serpent seductively whispered in our ear, "You can be like God. In fact, you can become God and take his place."

The devil tricked Adam and Eve, and they lost the perfect life they had in the Garden. Because of their disobedience, all of creation was plunged into the curse of sin and death. God responded to human arrogance and pride with judgment.

But in Acts 2, we see something quite different. Pentecost shows a new wind blowing, a wind of amazing grace. In Acts 2, we see how the judgment of Babel has been reversed. The curse has been broken. The day of mercy has arrived!

Peter told the people in Jerusalem that the Holy Spirit has now come to do something wonderful and new. All these signs and wonders of Pentecost are proof that God has indeed raised Jesus from the dead. God has made him Lord and Christ. The giving of the Holy Spirit was a sign of a new beginning for all of humanity.

Notice the differences between Genesis 11 and Acts 2. Babel showed a spirit of arrogance. Pentecost showed a spirit of grace. Babel divided people through different languages. Pentecost united them with the gift that broke past language barriers. Babel was about confusion, Pentecost was about coming together. Babel showed people full of themselves. Pentecost showed people full of the Holy Spirit.

Now, there is one common thing between these two events. After each event, the people were scattered. But the motives were completely different.

The people of Babel were scattered out of judgment. But after Pentecost, the believers were scattered to share the amazing grace of God. They were sent forth to become obedient witnesses and humble servants.

And, in the years to come, Christians would scatter over the entire Roman Empire, even going forth to Africa, India, Europe, and Asia.

The early Christians realized that the Holy Spirit was like a mighty, rushing wind which magnificently cleared the air, freeing everyone from the old way of life. The Spirit's arrival at Pentecost was a breath of fresh air. It transformed the way we look at our life and the way we relate to God.

Pentecost shows that God can erase the mistakes of the past. He can set us free to live a new life. We are not prisoners of our past. Like John Newton, we have been changed by God's amazing grace. The Holy Spirit has opened our eyes to see the power of the cross of Jesus.

At the main entrance to the Army Training Camp at Fort Dix, New Jersey, there is a large box with a big hole on top. As the new recruits approach the camp, they can drop in that box, with no questions asked, any illegal substance: drugs, alcohol, knives, guns, anything at all - and begin a new life in the army.

That's the way God works, too. The Holy Spirit leads us to the cross of Jesus and he takes all of our sins and he puts in the box of the Crucified Savior. Our sins are put away forever, and now, we are able to begin a new life in Christ.

In fact, when you look at the ministry of Jesus, you see how his mission was to give hope to the discouraged, to give freedom to the captives, to give healing to the hurting. Christ preached that Holy Spirit creates a new life in our hearts. The Holy Spirit is the God of second chances.

We all know what it's like to be discouraged and down. Sometimes, we feel trapped in our sinful ways. We all know that lost feeling, that guilty conscience, that broken heart, that feeling of shame and disgrace.

But listen, today God has a breath of fresh air for you. You are forgiven! You are spiritually healed and renewed! You have hope!

You are filled with the Holy Spirit. And now you can become an obedient witness to the Risen Savior and a humble servant to others. God can use you to draw people closer to him.

That's the breath of fresh air that Pentecost brings into our life. The Holy Spirit leads us to Christ. Through the power of his cross, we can let go of our efforts to try to make a great name for ourselves. We can stop trying to storm the gates of heaven. We can give up our arrogance and pride, and we can humbly receive the amazing grace of God.

A businessman tells the story of a big waterfront warehouse he was selling. The building had been empty for months and needed repairs. Vandals had broken down the doors, smashed the windows, and thrown trash all around the interior.

As he showed the warehouse to a prospective buyer, the businessman took pains to say that he would replace the broken doors and windows, and bring in a crew to correct any structural damage, and clean out the garbage, and so on.

"Forget about the repairs," the buyer said. "When I buy this place, I'm going to build something completely different here. I don't want the building. I want the site."

In the same way, we may try to change our lives and clean them up by our own power. But God has bigger plans. God wants to make all things new from the ground up. He wants to send a breath of fresh air into our hearts. He wants to change our life forever.

And through the power of Pentecost, we can become true servants of God, people who reach out to others with love and compassion, people who rejoice in the gift of the Holy Spirit. We can become people who love and serve others every day as we rejoice in the amazing grace of God. Amen!

THE COMFORT WE ALL NEED:
Isaiah 40:1-11

We begin today with Isaiah seeing a day when God would speak tenderly to his people. Isaiah says, "This is what God says, 'Comfort, comfort my people. Speak tenderly to Jerusalem and say to her that her conflict is ended. Her sins are pardoned.'"

Now Israel certainly did not deserve to be pardoned. The people had been unfaithful to God. They had compromised their faith and had turned away from the Lord who had saved them. They were worshipping and serving other gods.

Yet, Isaiah sees a time when God would speak tenderly to his people. God would say, "Comfort my people. Tell them their sin is pardoned, their unfaithfulness is forgiven." This is good news! This is the gospel. This is the comfort we all need.

Isaiah gives many words of comfort in his book. This is especially true when he speaks of the coming Messiah, the one who would be born of the virgin, the one who would be called "Immanuel," God with us.

Isaiah says the Messiah will be our King, a branch from the stump of Jesse. He would be anointed with the Holy Spirit. He would be the royal Son of David.

Yet, our Messiah King would also humble himself. Isaiah also describes him as the Suffering Servant of the Lord. He is the one who is smitten, stricken and afflicted. He is numbered among the transgressors. Our King is crucified on a cross. He wears a crown of thorns and dies as "The King of the Jews."

However, in the end, he rises from the dead. The glory of the Lord is revealed as the Messiah proves to be victorious over sin and death. Our King is vindicated and exalted.

And it all starts with a voice that cries out, "In the wilderness prepare the way of the Lord, make straight in the desert a highway for our God. Every valley shall be lifted up and every mountain made low. The uneven ground will become level and the rough places smooth."

Isaiah speaks of a messenger who will prepare the way of the Lord. He will be a solitary voice crying out in the dry desert, "Make a straight highway for our God."

John the Baptist fulfills this prophecy. He appeared in the wilderness of Judea, baptizing for the forgiveness of sins.

John proclaimed that the Messiah was at hand. "After me, comes one more powerful than I. He will straighten out what is crooked; he will heal what is broken. He will level out what is uneven."

Often, it seems like our life is pretty uneven. Our life is filled with potholes and broken ground. We keep hitting those rough spots. We are driving over broken pavement and cracked roads. That is why we experience such a rough, bumpy ride. Life is not easy. Everything seems crooked and warped.

Something is not quite right in our world. There is brokenness to our life, a deep crack we perceive and notice every day. And that's exactly how the Bible describes our fallen state.

Sin is brokenness. It is damage, corruption and decay. It is like a wooden board that has been warped by water damage. It is mold and rust and a rotting decay.

Sin is harmful and toxic, something intrinsically destructive to human life. Sin destroys and it brings pain, heartache, and tears.

Just ask the alcoholic, the drug addict, those in prison. Just watch the news and see the reports of shootings, terrorism, child abuse, murder, rape, domestic violence and other endless tragedies.

This fallen world is badly damaged. And when we drive down the road of life, it can get pretty bumpy. Sometimes, we can hardly hang on to the steering wheel. It gets pretty rough.

Crisis after crisis comes down the road. Sickness, suffering, health problems, family troubles, the death of loved ones – on and on it goes.

All these things are echoes of the fall. They are reminders that there once was a time when life was good and perfect. There once was a time when there was no sin or suffering or death. There were no tragedies or troubles.

But then, we rebelled against our Creator. We broke the promise of life. We were unfaithful and turned away from God. We brought death and brokenness into God's perfect creation.

But today, we hear a word of hope. "Look, I am sending my messenger before you who will prepare the way. He is the voice of one crying in the wilderness, 'Prepare the way of the Lord, and make his paths straight.'"

Prepare the way for the Lord. The Messiah is here! This is the gospel of Jesus Christ, the Son of God.

He has come to lift up every valley and to level out the uneven ground. He comes to heal our brokenness and to straighten out what is crooked. The Son of God comes to undo all the damage our rebellion has caused.

Isaiah says, "The glory of the Lord shall be revealed and all people will see it together. The mouth of the Lord has spoken." You do see the glory of God clearly revealed in the life of Jesus Christ.

And you especially see his glory in his miracles. Think about all those miracles of healing that Jesus worked. Here we clearly see how the Messiah comes to heal our brokenness. He comes to restore health and well-being and to fix what is damaged.

The Lord opens eyes that are blind, he causes the deaf to hear, he cleanses lepers, and he makes the paralyzed to walk again. Christ restores God's Creation. He lays his hand upon the sick and they are cured. What is crooked is straightened out and the rough places are made smooth.

Christ also brings forgiveness to lives that have been damaged by the effects of sin. The woman caught in adultery is forgiven. Zacchaeus, the tax collector who steals from the poor, is forgiven and turns away from his crooked ways. Christ forgives those who have fallen into the cracks and potholes of life: "Your sins are forgiven. Go in peace."

This is the comfort we all need. Isaiah says, "Go up on a high mountain and lift up your voice with strength. Proclaim the good news, 'Behold, your God had come! He has come to save you.'"

Imagine that! God himself comes to save us. God himself comes to rescue us from our bondage to sin and death. God himself comes to set us free from frustration and fear. God himself comes in the flesh.

The Son of God is born of the virgin Mary. He is Immanuel, God with us. He takes on our flesh and blood; he enters our life. In this way, the Lord takes our brokenness upon himself.

Isaiah speaks of what Christ has done for us. He says, "Surely he took our infirmities and carried our sorrow. He was pierced for our transgressions; he was crushed for our iniquities. The punishment that brought us peace was upon him, and by his wounds we are healed."

By his wounds, you are healed. Through his shed blood, your sins are forgiven. Our Lord's suffering and death on the cross brings a true healing. It brings an end to the broken road of potholes and cracked pavement. All of that is now covered by a new highway that leads straight to heaven, the new creation.

I think there's something delightful about a road that has been freshly paved and made like new. You can still smell the asphalt and tar. The road is brand new and fresh.

We all have to deal with all those highway and road construction projects that just seem endless. You have had to slow down and carefully drive through the construction zones. Sometimes, the road is all broken up. You drive over the rough spots and go through the detours.

Finally, the highway-paving project is done and you have a brand new road that is smooth, level and flawless. You finally get to drive over the finished project. And that's how it will be in God's kingdom.

Our Lord's cross and resurrection bring about a new highway construction project. God is now busy and hard at work in this construction zone. The Holy Spirit is now leveling out the rough spots of our life. The valleys are filled in. The mountains are made low. The uneven ground becomes level; the broken ground is made right.

The Holy Spirit totally renovates our heart and soul. He paves over our sins with the cross and resurrection of Christ. He rebuilds us through the power of God's love.

"Comfort, comfort my people," says your God. "Speak tenderly to them and say, 'Your sins are forgiven.'"

The Lord God speaks to us today and he says, "Believe in the good news that I love you! Believe that I will help you through the rough spots you are going through. I will comfort you with my power and grace. But continue to follow my highway. Keep on believing and you will see the glory of heaven revealed."

God bestows his comfort upon us, and we are now able to share that gift with other people. They also need to discover that comforting message of Jesus Christ, the Son of God.

Listen: you can comfort someone with the comfort you have received from God. You can say to someone who is hurting and bruised in spirit, "Christ is the one who loves you with an everlasting love. His love is powerful and strong and the Lord will help you in your time of need."

"Love is the Key!" Go now in peace and continue to serve the Lord. Continue to share the comfort we all need. Amen!

ARE YOU READY? Mark 13:24-37

Do you know what is truly amazing? Do you know what totally surprises me? Despite what Jesus clearly says, many people have insisted on predicting the date of his second coming. They try to predict the last day. However, Jesus clearly says, "No one knows about that day or hour, not even the angels in heaven, nor the Son, but only the Father." No one knows when that time will come.

Now, there is no doubt. People are definitely fascinated with what the Bible teaches about the end times. We all want to learn more about the end of the world. However, some go beyond what the Scriptures teach. They come up with complicated schemes and timetables, usually based on Daniel and Revelation.

It seems like there is always somebody somewhere who has figured out when the final countdown will begin. Does anybody here remember Y2K? Or what about the Mayan calendar which supposedly predicted the end of the world in 2012?

I think all this happens because people are worried about the future. The world is falling apart and we are looking for something to hold on to. Things are getting crazy. We want reassurance that God is still in control.

That is why there is such a great appeal in trying to predict when the last day will come. It gives people reassurance to think they have an inside track on God's plan. However, we really don't need complicated schemes or timetables in order to be reassured. We don't need to figure out who the Antichrist is, or where the ten-toed kingdom of Daniel is located, or what being "left behind" means.

The end-time teaching of the Bible is pretty straightforward and direct. We just confessed it in the Apostles' Creed. "Christ will come again to judge the living and the dead. I believe in the forgiveness of sins, the resurrection of the body and the life everlasting."

When the Lord comes again to this world on the last day, he will come openly and visibly to all people. "At that time men will see the Son of Man coming in clouds with great power and glory." When Christ comes again, all the dead will be raised up. Everyone will then be judged. All those who believe in Christ will receive the crown of life. They will enter the life everlasting and will experience God's new creation, the renewed heavens and earth.

That is why we look forward to the second coming of Christ. For us, it will be a day of great joy and gladness. It will be a day of glory and triumph. It will be a day of meeting our Savior face-to-face and being reunited with our loved ones and friends. This is our hope – this is what will know will happen on the last day.

Now, let us play a little game for a moment. Let's just suppose that somehow we discovered that Jesus will be coming tomorrow. Let's say that Christ is definitely coming tomorrow. What would you do?

Think about it. If everybody knew that tomorrow was the last day, what do you think people would do? Some would probably care less. They would just tune-out and ignore the whole thing. Some would probably have a big party. "Hey, let's go out with a bang! Let us eat and drink and be merry for tomorrow we die."

Others would probably be devastated at the thought of losing everything they had worked so hard for. I mean, just think – all of your money and savings, all of your possessions and belongs – your car, your house, your retirement account – all gone! Here we are reminded that there is more to this life than just having money and possessions. We brought nothing into this world and we take nothing out of it either.

So again, the question before us is this: "What would you do if tomorrow were the last day?"

Martin Luther gave a famous answer to this question. A friend once asked Luther, "What would you do if you found out tomorrow was the last day?" Luther thought for a moment and answered, "I would probably work in my garden. I would plant an apple tree or do something like that." His friend said, "Really?" And Luther said, "Yes, I would. Do you know why? Because God would want me to do something constructive and positive. God would want me to live out my faith, no matter what the circumstances."

Luther's answer reminds us that today is the only day we have. You can't live in the past. You can't live in the future. Today is the only day you have. So, live out your faith today! Do something positive and constructive with your life right now.

Remember, each of us has a calling. Each of us has our specific assigned task, both in God's kingdom and in our daily life. And when we carry out our task, we are being faithful servants, servants who are prepared, ready, and watchful for the Lord's return.

Jesus says, "It is like a man going away on a journey. He leaves his house and puts his servants in charge while he is away. They each have their assigned task." In essence, our Lord says, "The best way to be prepared for the end is to have faith and to live out that faith each day."

Notice how Jesus compares his ascension into heaven to a man going away on a journey. Our Lord leaves his house and he puts us in charge, each with our assigned task. Each of us has a specific task, a calling, a job to do. We all have a responsibility to serve the Lord and to serve other people.

We all have a job to do. Now is the time to wake up and get to work. Today is the day to show mercy and compassion to all we meet. Now is the time to share the gospel. Now is the time to love and give and to share your life with others. Live in love and service to all.

Through faith in Jesus Christ, we all become his servants. Remember, he is the one who suffered and died and rose again for you. He died on the cross for your sins and rose again from the dead so that you might have the forgiveness of sins, the resurrection of the body and the life everlasting.

Through faith in Christ, you can face the future with confidence and hope. You can be strong even in these difficult times. You can be reassured that God is still in control. The Son of God is your foundation and strength. He is your Savior, your Lord, your King.

And even if tomorrow were your last day, you have the confidence of knowing that there is life after death. A new and better life awaits you when you die. This is our confidence and hope. "I believe in the resurrection of the body and the life everlasting."

Therefore, have faith in Christ and put your faith into action. Go and serve the Lord! Go and share the gospel! Go and love others! Go and reach to everyone in mercy and compassion. Share the hope that you have in Christ with others.

Have faith in Christ and trust that your Savior will soon return. Be that faithful servant who watches and prays for his return. Be faithful, watch and pray, and rejoice! Through faith in Christ, you are now ready for his return. Amen!

A CHOICE TO MAKE: Matthew 2:1-12

It was not a peaceful night in the palace of King Herod in Jerusalem. The king stormed around the throne room, muttering curses under his breath. Along the wall, his advisers were huddled in groups of two's and three's. Suddenly, the king stopped and addressed the religious leaders he had assembled.

"Well," he thundered. "What about it?" The king gestured to some guests who had come from the east bearing strange tidings. They had come to King Herod and had asked, "Where is the one who has been born the king of the Jews? We have seen his star and have come to worship him."

"Well?" said Herod. "What do they mean? They ask for a king and they don't mean me! I what to know - who is this supposed king, and where can he be found?"

The religious leaders and advisers looked at each other with raised eyebrows. Finally, one of them mustered his courage to speak. He said, "O king, the Messiah is to be born in Bethlehem for this is what the prophet Micah has written, 'But you, O Bethlehem in the land of Judah are by no means least among the clans of Judah, for out of you will come a ruler who will be the shepherd of my people Israel.'"

"All right, that is all!" Herod growled. "You are dismissed. Leave me now."

Then, Herod directed his visitors from the east into a side room. He took a deep breath and made an effort to suppress his anger. "Gentlemen," he began quietly, "Tell me, when did you see this star appear? And how is it that you are you so interested in seeking out this king?"

One of the visitors answered, "Sir, we are students of the stars and also students of your religion. We have learned to read your Holy Scriptures because your people were brought to our land of Persia many centuries ago when the Babylonians sent your people into exile."

"We have studied the books of Moses and we know that it is written, 'A star shall come out of Jacob,' and 'The scepter will not depart from Judah nor the ruler's staff until Shiloh comes.'"

"Furthermore, King Herod, we have learned that when this king comes, he will shepherd his people Israel and will bring them peace and salvation, a salvation that will extend to all the peoples of the earth! This is the king we have come to worship because we have seen his star arise out of Jacob."

"Well, I see," Herod replied. "So, the King of Israel has been born. The Messiah has finally come, has he? If that is the case, please go and find this child so that I may go and worship him as well."

Then, the visitors from the east set forth. They travelled down to Bethlehem (which is south of Jerusalem). However, they never returned or came back.

And so now, Herod faced a choice. What would he do concerning this rival king? Herod must now choose between protecting his own power or worshipping this newborn king.

But another king Herod could never tolerate; therefore, he must eliminate him. He must preserve his own rule. This king must die. Herod's choice was a hateful rejection.

But Matthew tells us that the Magi chose very differently. Their choice was a humble worship of this newborn King of Israel. They followed the way of the star, came to the house and saw the child with his mother Mary. They then they bowed down and worshipped him.

They opened their hearts and their treasures to him. They gave their gifts and gave their lives to the Lord. They bowed down to worship this child promised by God so long ago. We can certainly identify with these worshipping Magi.

However, let's be aware - there is a little bit of Herod in all of our hearts. Sometimes, we too resist this king who would come into our hearts. We resist and reject his claim on our lives.

Very often, we refuse to submit to our newborn king. We oppose the Lord Christ because we want to be king. We want to rule our own lives and do whatever we desire. We don't want anyone telling us what to do. We do not want to obey the Word of God. We would rather live in sin and rebellion against God.

Now, it is interesting that Matthew records another reaction to the news of the Messiah's coming. Consider the reaction of the chief priests and scribes. They also faced a choice.

The religious leaders of Jerusalem knew exactly what the wise men were talking about. They know who they were looking for. They even knew where the Messiah could be found.

But they did not go to Bethlehem. They did not go to search for this newborn king. They stayed in Jerusalem. I have always wondered about that.

It seems like they just didn't care. They knew what the prophets wrote concerning where the Christ was to be born, but they were filled with gross indifference. They were apathetic and could have cared less.

Many people are like this today. They may know all about Jesus, they may know all about what the Bible teaches and they may even belong to a church – but they really could care less about the things of God. They are too busy with work or sports or having a good time. They have no time for worship or reading God's Word or following the Lord Jesus.

Sometimes, we too fall into that trap. We take our Lord for granted and we neglect his Word. We don't follow his way. We close our hearts to him and refuse to bow down and worship our king.

This too is an opposition to the Lord Christ. It is a rejection of the king who wants to come into our life. The Lord wants to claim your life as his very own. He wants to be your Savior, Lord and King.

And here, we are faced with a choice. Either we fully accept the Lord Christ as our King or we reject him. There is no middle way. Either you follow Christ or you don't. Either you worship the Christ and believe in him, or you oppose the Christ and reject him.

As the rest of Matthew's Gospel reveals, the Lord Christ encountered increasingly violent opposition as he carried out his ministry. The religious leaders of Jerusalem would eventually prove to be just as ruthless and murderous as evil King Herod.

In the end, they would conspire to crucify an innocent man. They would reject the promised Messiah. Shiloh would come to them, but they would not believe in him. The King of the Jews would wear a crown of thorns and die on a cross. But all of this was already evident at the very beginning. The cross was already overshadowing the Magi's visit to Bethlehem.

Already, as the Magi gathered to worship the Christ-child, the cross looms like a dark shadow. King Herod will now seek to destroy this child. He will send his soldiers to Bethlehem to kill all the baby boys. Jesus and his parents must now flee to Egypt to save their lives.

My point is that we often think that Jesus suffered only during his crucifixion. However, we should remember that already as a child, he was enduring danger, opposition and hardship. Already, even as a baby, he was suffering for us. Jesus suffered his entire life.

This is our Messiah King who willingly endures all things for our salvation. He is totally obedient to the Father, even from birth. The King of the Jews comes to rescue us from darkness and death. He comes to suffer and die.

He suffers and dies for all those who reject and oppose him. He suffers and dies for us. It is for us that he cries out, "Father, forgive them!

Father, forgive them for they know not what they do."

Such forgiveness changes our hearts. Our King shines the light of his grace upon us and the darkness flees. His love shines like a star and we are once again led to his manger.

Look again and see! From the manger comes the warm glow of his shining light. This bright and brilliant light radiates from the Son of God. He is the King of Kings and the Lord of Lords. His light gives warmth and comfort and peace.

This is God's light, a light that removes the darkness from our hearts. Now, we no longer oppose the Lord or take him for granted. Christ comes into our hearts and he gives us the gift of the Holy Spirit.

The Holy Spirit now kindles the light of saving faith in our hearts. The Spirit of God helps us to follow our King. The Spirit enables us to make the right choice. Now, we join the wise men in kneeling down before the Savior and worshipping him.

We join the wise men today as we worship the Christ-child. We open our hearts and our treasures. We once again offer our gifts and ourselves to the Lord Christ. We joyfully bow down before our glorious King, Jesus Christ, the Son of God. Amen!

Here's a bonus sermon from the book

God's Punch Line

GOD'S PUNCH LINE: Luke 24:1-12

Today, we remember that Easter is a time for joy and laughter. After the seriousness of Lent, and all the heaviness of Holy Week, Easter is a time to lighten up and smile. It is a time to enjoy God's punch line.

For example, Joseph of Arimathea was a wealthy Pharisee, a member of the Jewish ruling council and a secret follower of Jesus. It was Joseph who went to Pilate and asked for the body of Jesus after the crucifixion. He also supplied his own tomb for our Lord's burial.

Well, the story is told that someone pulled Joseph aside and said, "Joseph that was such beautiful, expensive, hand-carved tomb. Why on earth would you give it to someone else to be buried in?" Joseph just smiled, and said, "Why not? He only needed it for the weekend!"

Christ's resurrection is God's joke on the devil, and I bet the devil must have been pretty surprised to find that the tomb was empty. The power of death could not hold the Son of God.

In our reading for today, Luke shows that the resurrection was God's joke on the disciples, too. The women didn't expect what they found, and the men didn't believe what the women told them, and Peter himself was completely puzzled by what had happened.

It was an astonishing turn of events. Luke says that the women went to the tomb early on Sunday morning. They found the tomb open and they went inside.

The angels greeted them with the question, "Why do you look for the living among the dead? He is not here. He has risen! Remember how he told you, 'The Son of Man must be delivered into the hands of sinful men, be crucified and on the third day be raised again.'"

The women were completely amazed at the message the angels delivered. In the same way, the apostles were clueless about what had really happened, and Peter was left wondering to himself what had occurred. Here, we see three different reactions.

In the Bible, three is an important number. Three establishes a pattern. It is the number of completeness. We confess our faith in the three persons of the Trinity - the Father, the Son, and the Holy Spirit.

Three wise men visited the baby Jesus after he was born. Jesus took three disciples with him up to the Mount of Transfiguration (and also inside the Garden of Gethsemane). Peter denied Jesus three times. Three men were crucified on Good Friday. Christ rose from dead on the third day. We could go on.

And have you ever noticed that in many jokes, the third person often provides the punch line? For example: three men die and they find themselves at the pearly gates of heaven. St. Peter tells them that they can enter heaven, if they can answer but one simple question.

Peter asks the first man, "What is Easter?" The man replies, "Oh, that's easy. It's that holiday in November when everybody gets together, eats turkey, and watches football."

Peter shakes his head, and goes on to the second man. He asks him the very same question, "What is Easter?" The man replies, "Easter is that big holiday in December when we put up a nice tree, exchange presents, and celebrate the birth of Jesus."

Peter then goes up to the third man, and again asks, "What is Easter?" This man smiles, looks Peter squarely in the eye and says, "Easter is the holiday where remember how Jesus was betrayed and turned over to the Romans by one of his own disciples. They sentenced him to be crucified, made him wear a crown of thorns and hung him on a cross. He died and was buried in a nearby tomb which was sealed off by a large stone."

Peter smiles with delight. But then, the man continued, "Every year the stone is moved aside, so that Jesus can come out, and if he sees his shadow, there will be six more weeks of winter."

You see, it's the third person who provides the punch line here. Three is an important number. And looking back through the Gospel of Luke, we find three accounts of people being raised from the dead. Three resurrections, but the third one delivers God's punch line.

In chapter seven, Luke gives us the account of Jesus raising the widow's son at the town of Nain. While traveling about in his ministry of teaching and healing, Jesus encounters a widow leading the funeral procession of her only son.

Luke says that Jesus had compassion on this widow. When he saw her weeping, his heart went out to her and he said, "Do not cry." Then, the Lord went up and touched the coffin and those who were carrying it stood still. (It was an open casket, so to speak, a funeral bier.)

Jesus then said, "Young man, I say to you, get up!" And the young man sat up and began to speak. The Lord helped him down from the coffin and gave him back to his mother.

In chapter eight, Jesus raised the daughter of Jairus, the synagogue ruler. Jairus had asked Jesus to come to his house to heal his daughter, but she died before the Lord could arrive. Someone came from the house of Jairus and said, "Your daughter is dead. Don't bother the teacher anymore."

But upon hearing this, Jesus said to Jairus, "Do not be afraid; just believe, and she will be healed." Some people laughed at him, knowing that she was dead. But Jesus went up to her room, and he took her by the hand and said, "Little girl, I say to you, get up!" At once she got up, alive. Jesus then told them to give her something to eat.

And now, in chapter 24, our reading for today, we have the account of our Lord's resurrection. This, of course, is God's great punch line to the entire world.

The resurrection of Jesus is God's punch line, and it declares that everything has now completely changed. God's saving work is done. The great turning point of all history has occurred.

Do you remember what the angels told the women at the tomb? The angels said, "Why do you look for the living among the dead? He is not here; he has risen! Remember how he told you, 'The Son of Man must be crucified and on the third day be raised again.'"

Luke specifically says, "Then, the women remembered the words of Jesus." Then, it all clicked together. Then, they got the punch line. The words of Christ made sense. It was all true! His promises are sure! When the Lord says something in his Word, you can believe it with all of your heart and soul.

It was necessary for the Son of Man to be delivered over into death. He had to be crucified. He had to deal with our sin problem, and take all of our guilt upon himself. He had to give himself into such suffering and death, so that we might receive forgiveness.

Jesus had to die on that cross for us and be buried in the tomb. But, on the third day, he was raised to life. That resurrection of Jesus changes everything.

Now, a new life begins for us. This is not our old life of weakness and failure. It is a new life of faith and hope, conviction and courage. It is that life which begins in the waters of Holy Baptism.

Baptism bestows life and salvation. We are born again by water and the Word. The Holy Spirit gives life as he connects us to the cross and resurrection of Jesus.

In Baptism, the resurrection power of the Son of God flows into your life. God the Father accepts you as his child, and he declares, "My Son has risen from the dead, and he has risen for you. Because he lives, you too shall live."

And on the last day, our physical bodies will be raised from the dead and transformed to be like our Lord's glorified body. On that day, we will fully enter the perfect and complete life we all yearn for.

Then, our baptism into Christ will reach its completion as we are raised from the dead and glorified. That final resurrection we will experience on the last day is God's final punch line to the entire universe.

Then, we will begin to enjoy God's new creation. We will begin to experience complete peace, joy and happiness. We will smile and rejoice because we will have reached our final goal.

We all know that this current life we experience today is not what God originally intended for humanity. This life is often so difficult and hard. We all struggle with unhappiness and disappointment. We are filled with depression, worry and anxiety.

Sometimes we feel just like the widow of Nain or Jairus. We experience the loss of our loved ones and friends. Death hurts us deeply.

We weep our tears of sadness and grief. We are filled with pain and hurt.

But that is exactly why we need to remember the words and promises of Jesus. We need to remember that he says, "I am the resurrection and the life. Whoever believes in me has everlasting life."

"Come to me, all you who are weary and burdened, and I will give you rest. Take my yoke upon you and learn from me, for I am gentle and humble in heart. Come and you will find rest for your soul."

"Peace be with you. Why are you troubled and why do doubts arise in your minds? Look at my hands and feet. It is I myself! Touch me and see, a ghost does not have flesh and bones, as you see I have."

When the Risen Lord appeared to his followers after his resurrection, they finally got God's punch line. Before that, they were puzzled and confused. They were at a loss to make sense of what had occurred. They were totally clueless.

Often we are like that, too. We need to open our hearts to the Easter message, and then, everything will fall into place for us. Then we will understand God's purpose for our life and his entire creation. Our confusion and uncertainty will disappear.

Now, we look to Lord by faith, and we hear him say, "Don't be afraid; just believe. I say to you, get up! Enter the new life I have won for you through my suffering, death and resurrection."

Christ says, "Come now, rejoice and sing! Smile and laugh – everything's going to be alright in your life, because from here on, you and I are going to walk together. I am with you! I will never leave you or forsake you."

One final thought. Did you hear about the two Roman soldiers who were guarding the tomb of Jesus? The stone had been rolled away, and the tomb was revealed as empty. The one guard looked inside, and then he says to the other one, "Well, now there's only one thing that's certain – taxes."

In our world, taxes are a certainty (and that's no laughing matter). But just as certain, for all who believe in Jesus Christ, death has lost its sting. Death has been defeated and vanquished forever. No more tears! Death does not have the last laugh.

The last laugh belongs to God. And today, the Lord God says, "Why are looking for the living among the dead? My Son is not here; he has risen. Remember how he told you that all this was necessary. Remember how he told you."

That's the key - remember all the words Christ has spoken to you. Believe his promises with all your heart and soul. Believe and then you will experience the joy of a new life and the promise of the new creation to come.

Go ahead, smile. Rejoice and sing. The victory is yours! Christ has risen; he has risen, indeed. This is God's punch line delivered to you today. Amen!

However, Christ has indeed been raised from the dead, the first fruits of those who have fallen asleep. Since death came through a man, the resurrection of the dead comes also through a man.

As in Adam all die, so in Christ, all will be made alive. However, each in his own turn: Christ, the first fruits; then, when he comes, those who belong to him.

1 Corinthians 15:20-23

+

So then, just as you received Christ Jesus as Lord, continue to live in him, rooted and built up in him, strengthened in the faith as you were taught, and overflowing with thankfulness.

See to it that no one takes you captive through hollow and deceptive philosophy, which depends on human tradition and the basic principles of this world rather than on Christ.

For in Christ all the fullness of the Deity lives in bodily form, and you have been given fullness in Christ, who is the head over every power and authority.

Colossians 2:6-10

ABOUT THE AUTHOR:

Volker Heide graduated from the United States Merchant Marine Academy in Kings Point, New York in 1982. (B.S., Nautical Science) and worked in the offshore oil industry. He graduated from Concordia Seminary in St. Louis, Missouri in 1990. (M.Div., New Testament Theology).

He has been a parish pastor in the Lutheran Church – Missouri Synod for almost 30 years, and has served churches in Mississippi and Connecticut. He is married to his wife, Ellen, and they have two daughters, Melissa and Kristen.